I0472282

# contents

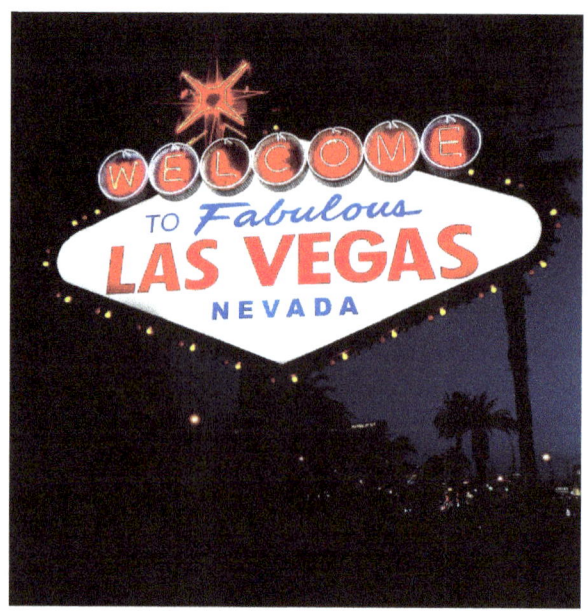

## Welcome to Fabulous Las Vegas

There are so many things to see, it's easy to get distracted. The bright lights and neon, the over-the-top attractions, casinos larger than any structures most of us have ever witnessed firsthand, Strip sideshows virtually everywhere you look, a man on the street who sits suspended in mid-air, sexy showgirls posing with tourists, the rush of water that bursts from the fountain up toward the open sky in front of the Bellagio, the tourists themselves, coming from all walks of life, the partygoers, the hopefuls. But just beneath all the showy glamour and glitz and often only feet from where Strip-goers revel in the spectacle is another world - a forgotten Las Vegas, hiding in plain sight.

Las Vegas is one of America's greatest cities. In fact, there is no other place like it in the world. It is a city of extremes. The world-famous Las Vegas Strip oozes ornate opulence, but just blocks from the bright lights are bedroom communities, sleepy in their mundane banality. A heat so intensely hot in the summer contrasts a chill that borders freezing in the winter. The big-city rush of the Strip, and just minutes away, the beautiful isolation of the mountainous desert and pristine Lake Mead. World-class dining experiences located adjacent to run-down, local food shacks. Tourists hyped up for their weekend getaway who hurriedly drive past locals just wanting to avoid the mania while they run their errands. This extremism helps keep the city exciting, vibrant and alive. But it's not the primary draw.

What is the true lure of Las Vegas? It's an escape from reality and, of course, gambling, winning money, and, hopefully, winning big. Money enables you to do the things you want to do, have the things you want to have. Money affords security, opportunity. And Las Vegas is built on that premise: the hope of money, the hope of opportunity. That hope in all of us is what keeps this city afloat as millions come every year with the hope they will win big. And sometimes, it happens. Often, it doesn't. These days, that hope transcends throughout all layers of the city. Hope for a resurgence, hope for a revival, hope for survival. During a very tough time in the city's history, this hope is what has kept Las Vegas alive.

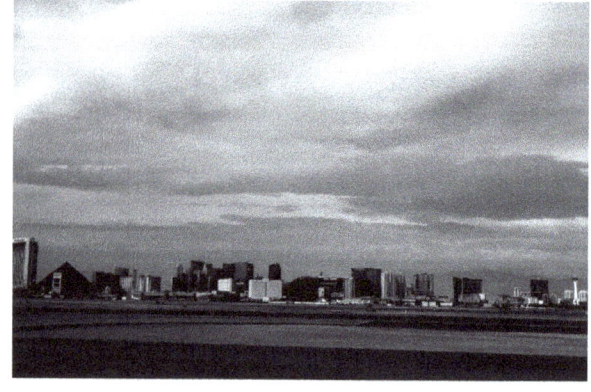

## Sin City Fallout

The year is now 2015, and it has been almost eight years since the onset of the Great Recession, which, according to the U.S. National Bureau of Economic Research (the official arbiter of U.S. recessions), began in the U.S. in December 2007 and ended in June 2009. Granted, many will argue it didn't begin until the market crash and Wall St. meltdown triggered by the investment bank collapses in 2008. Others who will likely dispute those exact dates are those who lost their jobs (and subsequently their homes) well after 2009 due to budget restraints caused by the Recession.

From the onset, Las Vegas was dealt a bad hand. By February 2009, a Forbes report cited Vegas as the no. 1 most abandoned city in America, based off Census Bureau statistics. It beat out Detroit at no. 2, followed by Atlanta. Sin City didn't hold the distinction long; Detroit eventually earned the top spot on the list of cities with the most vacant homes, and by 2013 Las Vegas had dropped down to no. 9.

But even now in 2015, some parts of town have an almost apocalyptic feel, where neglected buildings are left standing but there's no one around. And while it's more evident in some parts of town than others, it runs rampant throughout all of Las Vegas. You'd be hard-pressed to drive anywhere and not notice abandoned businesses, retailers, homes....everywhere. But most visitors will never know this, since they typically stay close to the Strip - and even the failed business ventures on the Strip are easily overlooked since most

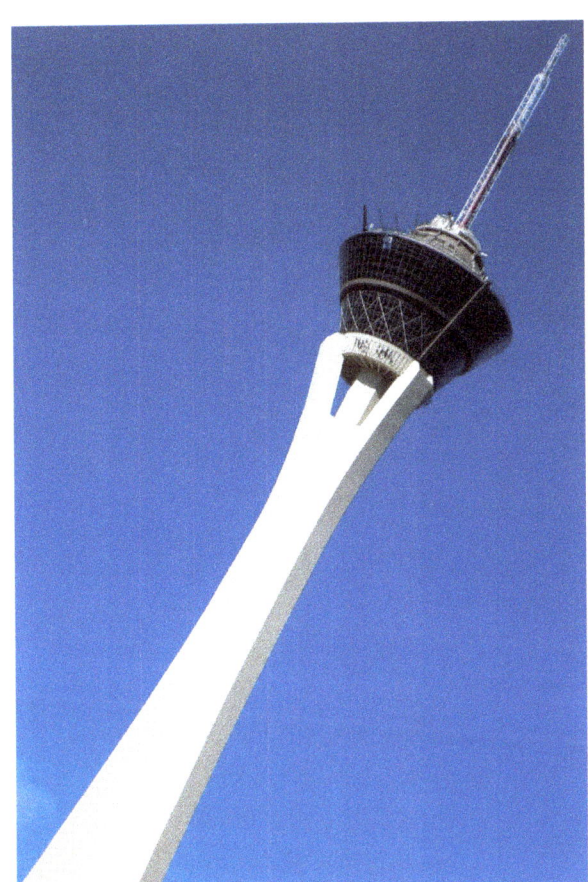

onlookers are distracted by the shiny objects.

The Recession affected everyone in this country. Some cities, more than others, were devastated. Eight years later, the economy has rebounded, companies are hiring again, city budget restrictions have been loosened, and things are slowly but surely going back to normal. But in some parts of the country, there are cities that were so badly affected by the Recession, the rebound has been a much slower process. Detroit is often cited as the poster child of a city ravaged by the financial collapse. Phoenix, parts of Florida, and, of course, often near the top of the list is Las Vegas. But why? How did this happen?

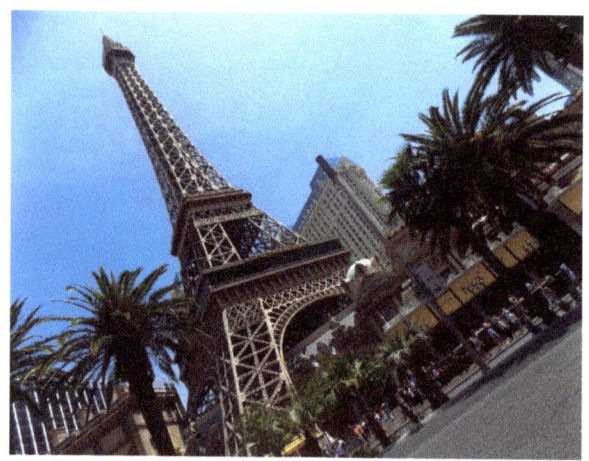

## What Happens in Vegas...

Since the late '90s, Vegas has been marketed as America's adult playground, the place to escape for a few days, really be yourself...or, be someone else. "What happens in Vegas, stays in Vegas." For many, it is like living a fantasy. But what most don't realize is that as the country's 30th largest city, with a population of around 600,000 in Las Vegas proper (or approximately 2 million when including the entire metro area), life for the people that live in Las Vegas is very real.

Gambling, tourism and the housing market are major drivers of the Las Vegas economy. Being that the housing crash was at the root of the Great Recession, Las Vegas was hit hard. So hard, in fact, that even as of 2015, Nevada is still listed as one of the states with the highest national average of foreclosed homes. RealtyTrac reported that in March 2015, Nevada had the second-highest foreclosure rate in the country and that 55 percent of foreclosed homes in Nevada were underwater (homeowners owe more than the house is actually worth) in the first quarter of 2015. (It's the highest rate in the country, the national average being 35 percent.)

Vegas, in particular, was strongly affected by the sub prime mortgage crisis, which was at the root of the crash. By now we all know about the less-than-stellar practices many financial institutions were engaging in during the 2000s, where they were not only issuing loans to people with poor credit or limited finances but were anticipating that most of those people would likely default on their loans.

And as for the state's economic health? A 2014 CNN Money report lists Nevada as the worst economy in the nation, down 10% from where it was in 2007. Much of this shortfall, the report says, is due to the loss of more than half its construction jobs. How about the availability of jobs critical for long-term growth? Of all U.S. states, Nevada comes in second-to-last place according to a February 2015 report from the Brookings Institute, with 5.1 percent of the national share of high-value jobs.

But it's not all bad news. According to Las Vegas-based Home Builders Research, there were 1,378 new home sales in Southern Nevada during the first quarter of 2015, up 8 percent from the first quarter of 2014. For the month of March, the median

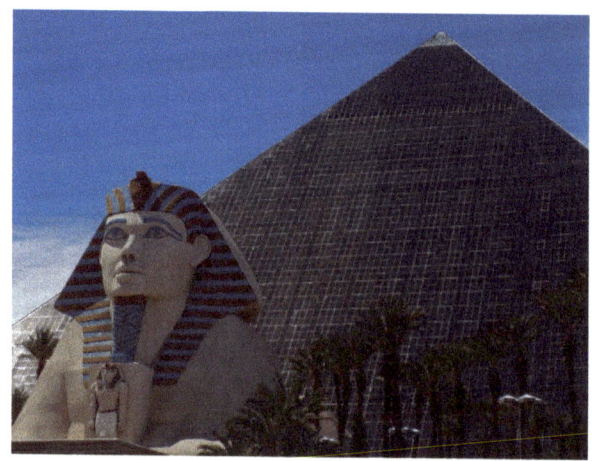

home sale price was $312,204, up 9 percent year-over-year. The housing market is always fluctuating, and Vegas has always been known for its volatile market, so things can always change.

Of course, these facts have not fallen on deaf ears with savvy investors, as now is an excellent time to buy property in the Las Vegas Valley, as buyers get way more home for their buck than in most other major cities. Considering the city's past as one of the fastest growing in the country, Vegas will bounce back. Now is as good a time as ever to get in on the ground floor (again).

**What Goes Up...**

What was really at the root of evil for Las Vegas stems back to the city's boom days in the 2000s.

When the census results came out in 2010, it was official: Las Vegas was the fastest growing major metropolitan city in America for the previous decade. The population of the Las Vegas metropolitan area (which includes Henderson, Boulder City, N. Las Vegas, Mesquite) had soared from roughly 1.4 million in 2000 to just over 2 million in 2010. (The most recent available stats from the U.S. Census Bureau showed a dip to 1,966,630 in 2011 and an uptick to 2,062,254 by 2013.) Forbes cited Las Vegas with a 14.9% job gain, giving it a job rank of 1. While it was all happening, the city was responding. Las Vegas knew its time had arrived. People were coming in droves, so the city expanded, developing new housing at a feverish pitch.

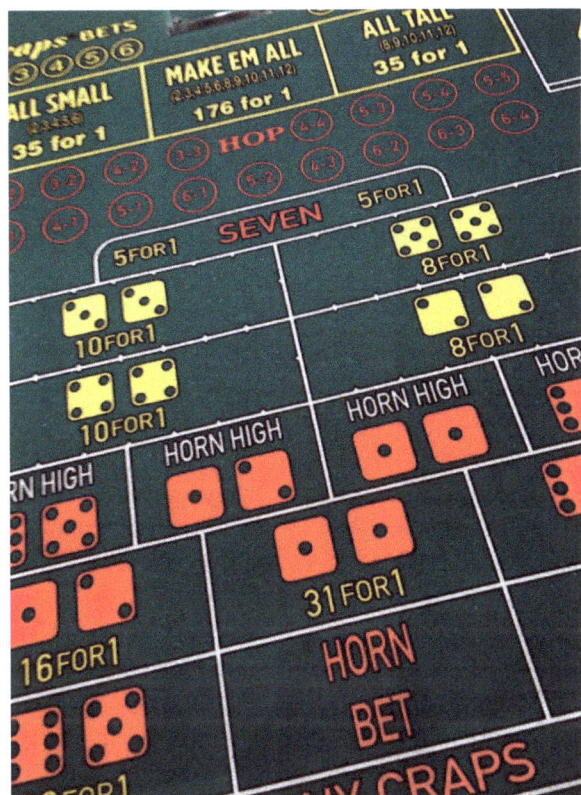

A 2006 comprehensive market analysis report from the U.S. Dept. of Housing and Urban Development cited Vegas as the fastest growing city in America. It was mostly young adults coming to work in the rapidly expanding service-providing sector of the local economy and retirees. The report added that over the next three years, there would be a demand for approximately 88,000 units of new sales housing and 18,000 new rental units. And jobs were way up. Employment growth in the gaming industry and related leisure and hospitality industries in 2005 had equaled the high levels recorded in the 1990s. So Vegas was building, fast and furious, to accommodate all those new people moving to the desert. But then, when the Recession hit, it all came to a crashing halt. Jobs were lost, homes were lost, tourism was way down, and the city was hurting.

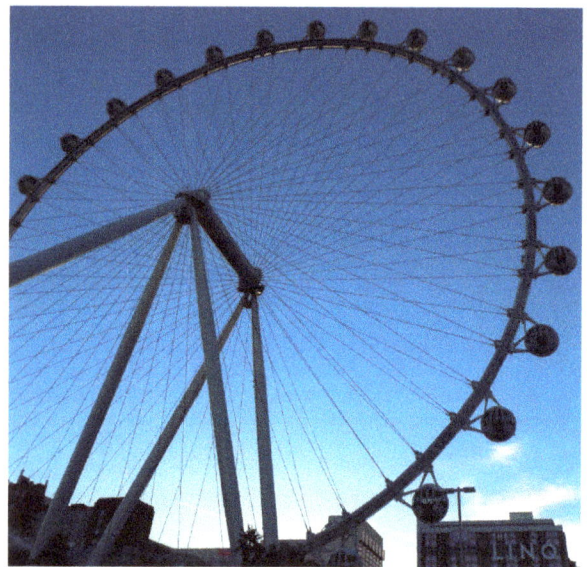

**Viva Las Vegas**

Eight years later, the city is still working hard to recover. Many have only heard or read about it, but to witness it firsthand is surreal: casino projects stalled, entire strip malls abandoned, residential construction halted and frozen in time, vacant homes, forgotten casinos and motels of days past...

And that is the purpose of this photography collection, shot in the first half of 2015. It's like your own private, guided tour, driving through abandoned Las Vegas. This collection is not intended to be comprehensive and doesn't include every single Sin City spot left behind. (After awhile, one abandoned grocery store starts to look a lot like the next, and there are only so many vacant fast food outlets and office plazas that can be accounted for in a single publication.)

This trip you are about to take will show how Las Vegas has been dramatically affected by the Great Recession. So sit back, relax and hopefully abandoned Las Vegas speaks to you, too. Because, after all, hope is what it's all about.

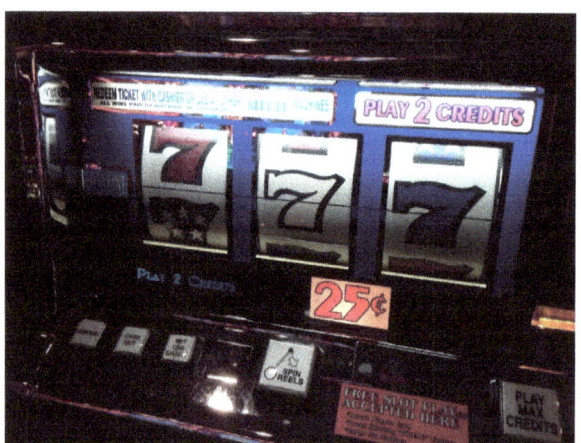

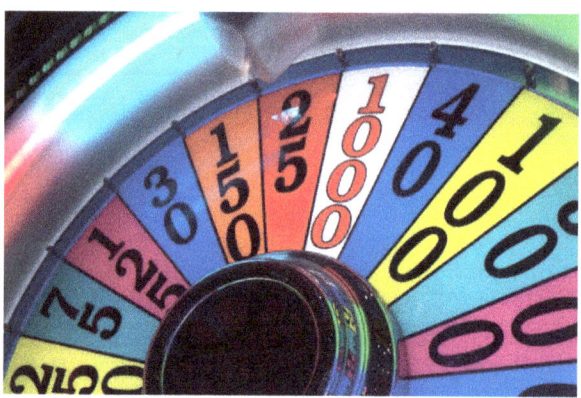

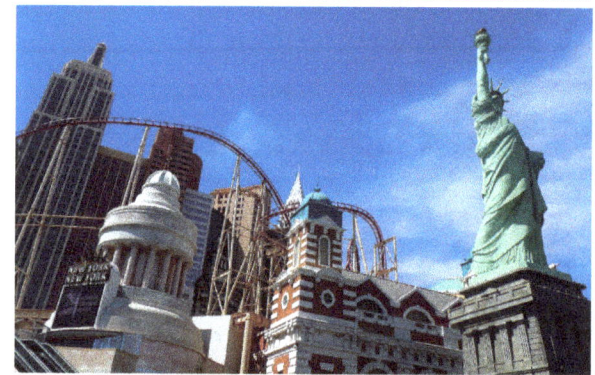

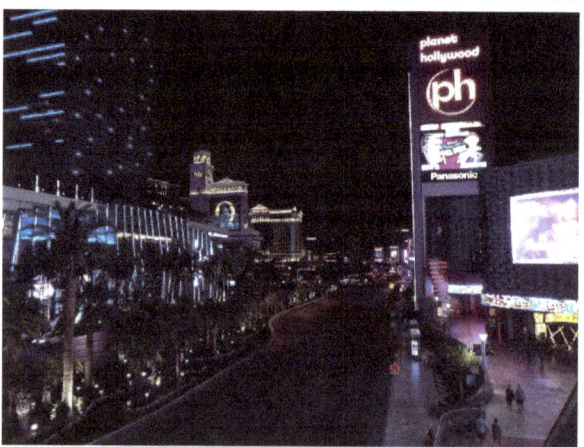

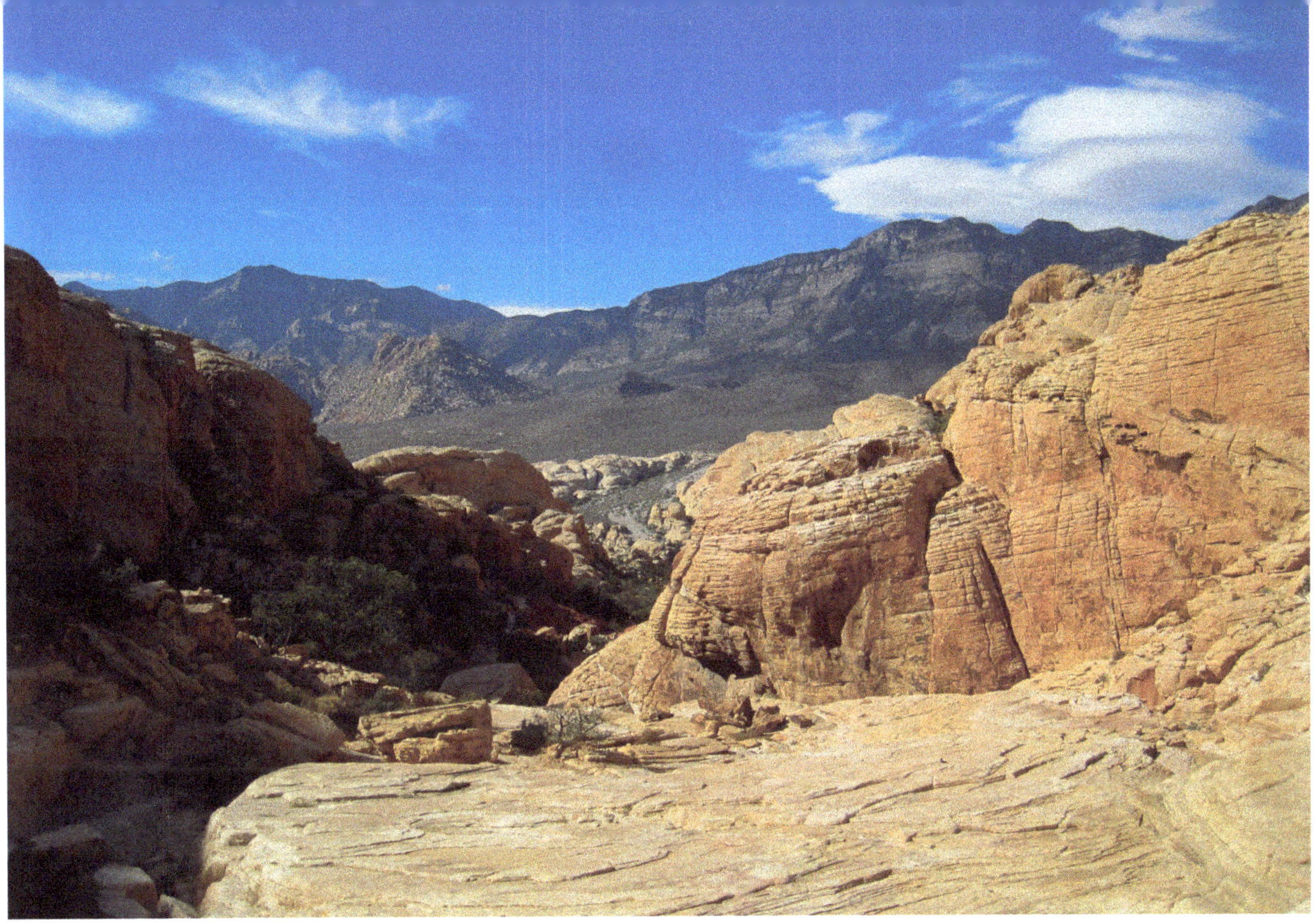

**Above:** Red Rock Canyon at Calico Tanks; **Below:** Lake Mead, Sunset View Overlook

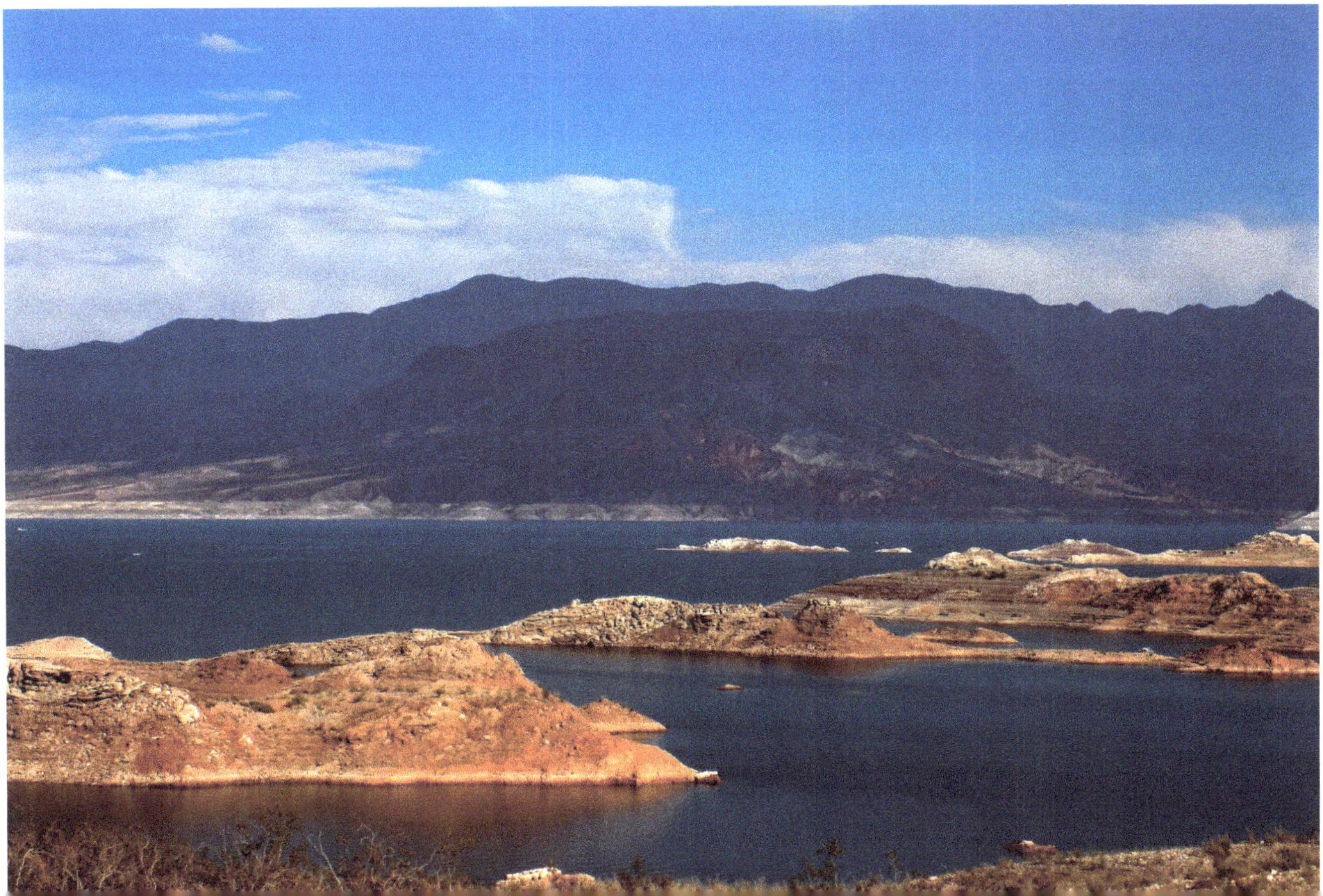

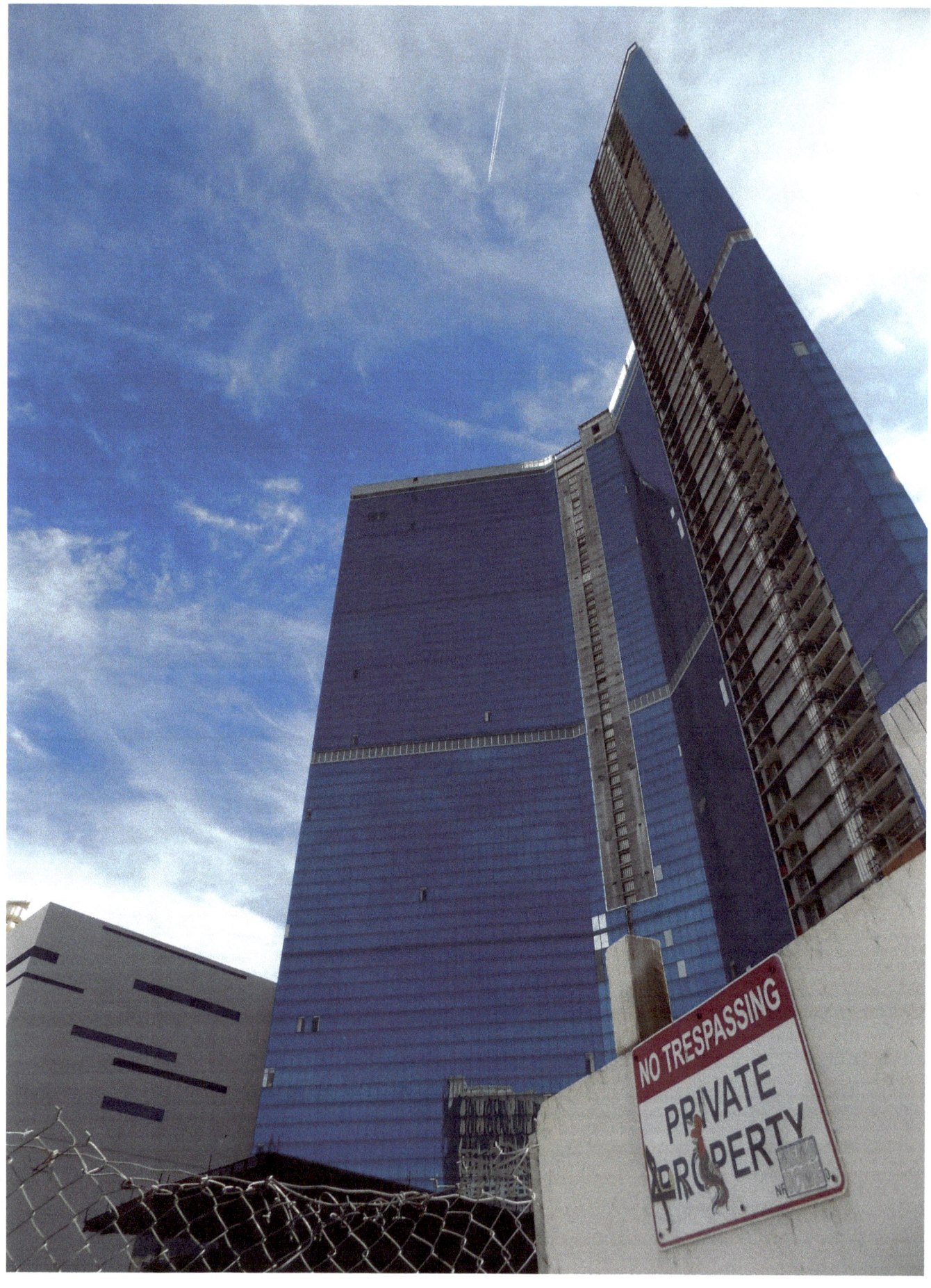

# *hiding in plain sight*

It almost seems that this chunk of land may be cursed. It has been over 10 years now since there have been any guests checking in or big wins at the tables on this property located near the North Strip.

Just south of Sahara Ave., at Riviera Blvd., the massive Fontainebleau Resort sits vacant on the 24.5 acre plot of land on the east side of Las Vegas Blvd. While it never even opened its doors, the uninhabited structure is the second-largest skyscraper in town. In June 2009, owners of the Fontainebleau filed for bankruptcy, and this empty and incomplete behemoth has continued ever since to loom over the Strip from behind construction barriers.

Situated between the new SLS Hotel & Casino (which opened in August 2014, replacing the Sahara Hotel & Casino) and the defunct Riviera Hotel & Casino (which closed its doors in May 2015), the Fontainebleau's 68-story hotel/casino/resort/condos complex sits on the former site of the El Rancho and Algiers hotels/casinos.

El Rancho closed in 1992 and sat boarded up until its implosion in 2000. The Algiers hotel shuttered 11 years ago in 2004, which was the last time this land saw any consumer activity. The parcel then sat inactive until April 2007, when groundbreaking on the Fontainebleau began.

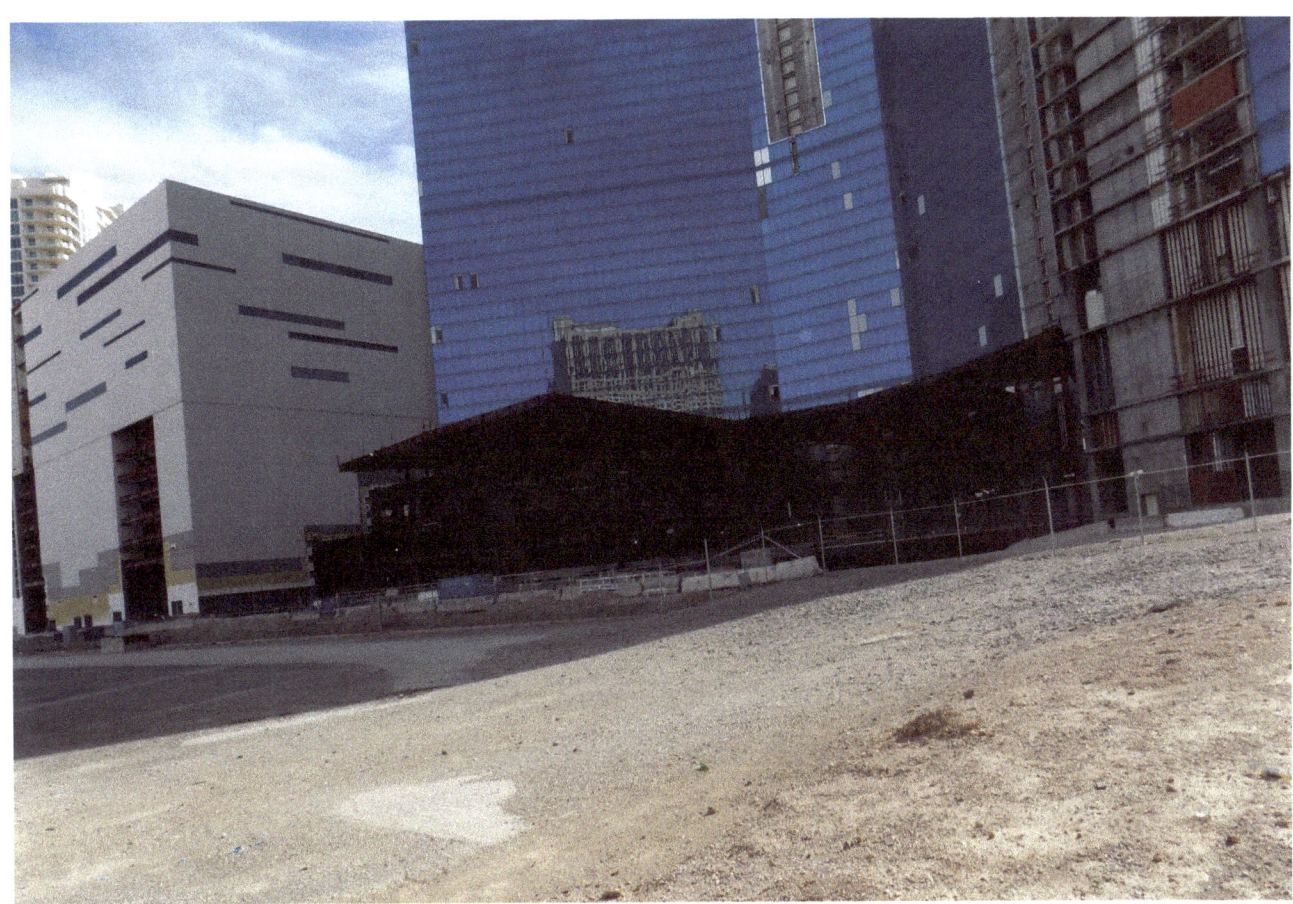

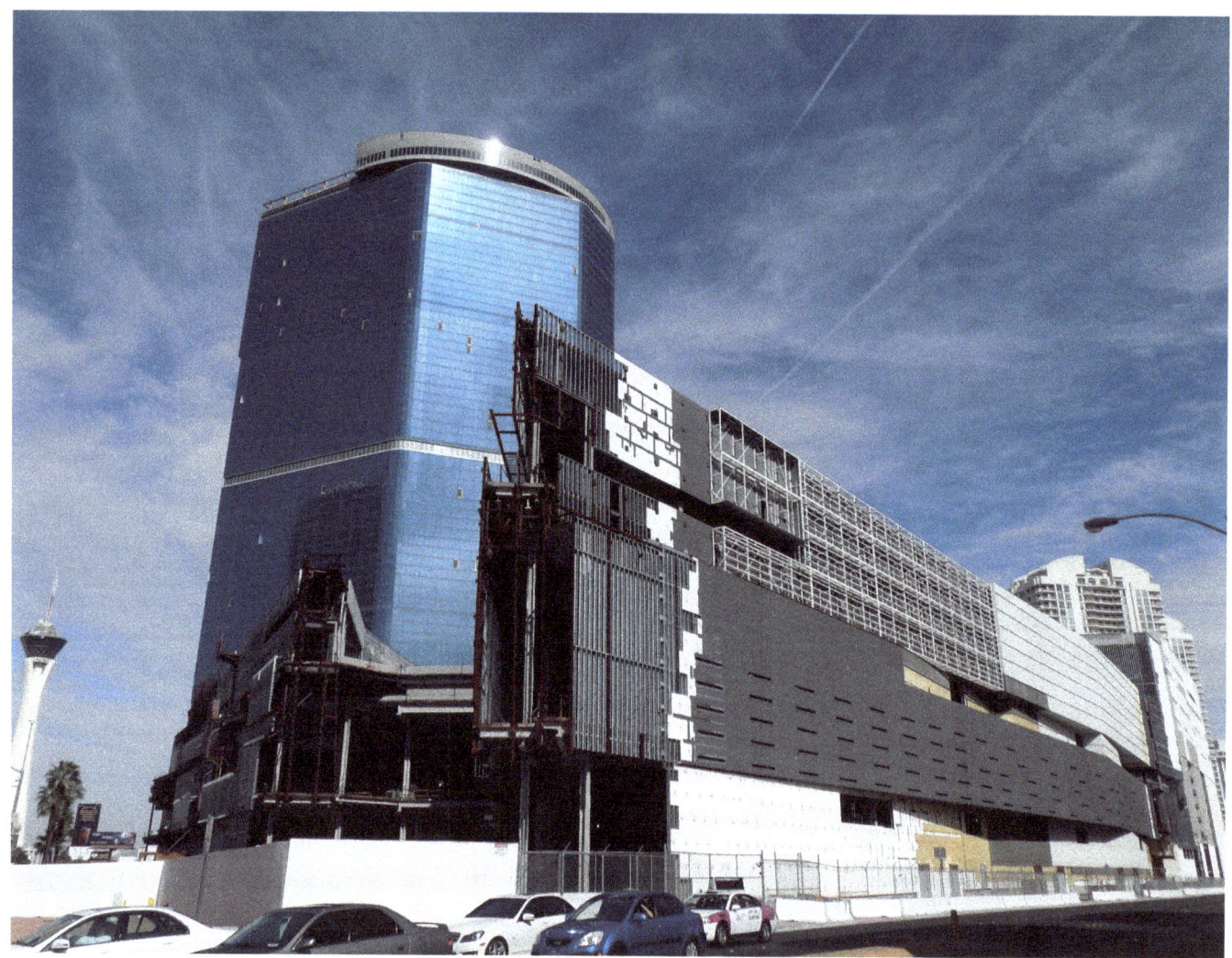

Prior to El Rancho's opening in 1981, it was home to the Thunderbird Hotel and Casino, which opened in 1948. The Thunderbird changed owners a handful of times over the years, and in 1977, when it was purchased by Major Riddle (owner of the Dunes), it received a facelift and a new name: the Silverbird, which it remained for approximately 4 years, when it changed hands again and became the El Rancho in '81.

The $2.9 billion Fontainebleau broke ground just a year before the market crash. It was originally slated to open its doors in October 2009 and was to include a 95,000 sq. ft. casino, 60,000 sq. ft. spa, 3,300-seat performing arts theater and 1,018 condo-hotel units, 180,000 sq. ft. of retail space, 400,000 sq. ft. of conference space, plus nightclubs and 24 restaurants and lounges. Financier Carl Icahn purchased the property in February 2010 for $156 mil. In August 2012, Morgan Stanley bought $320 million of Fontainebleau Las Vegas Holdings LLC's debt.

Sitting inactive now for six years, as of 2015, the future remains unclear for the Fontainebleau. Hiding in plain sight, it is a big-scale reminder of the struggles Las Vegas has faced during the Great Recession.

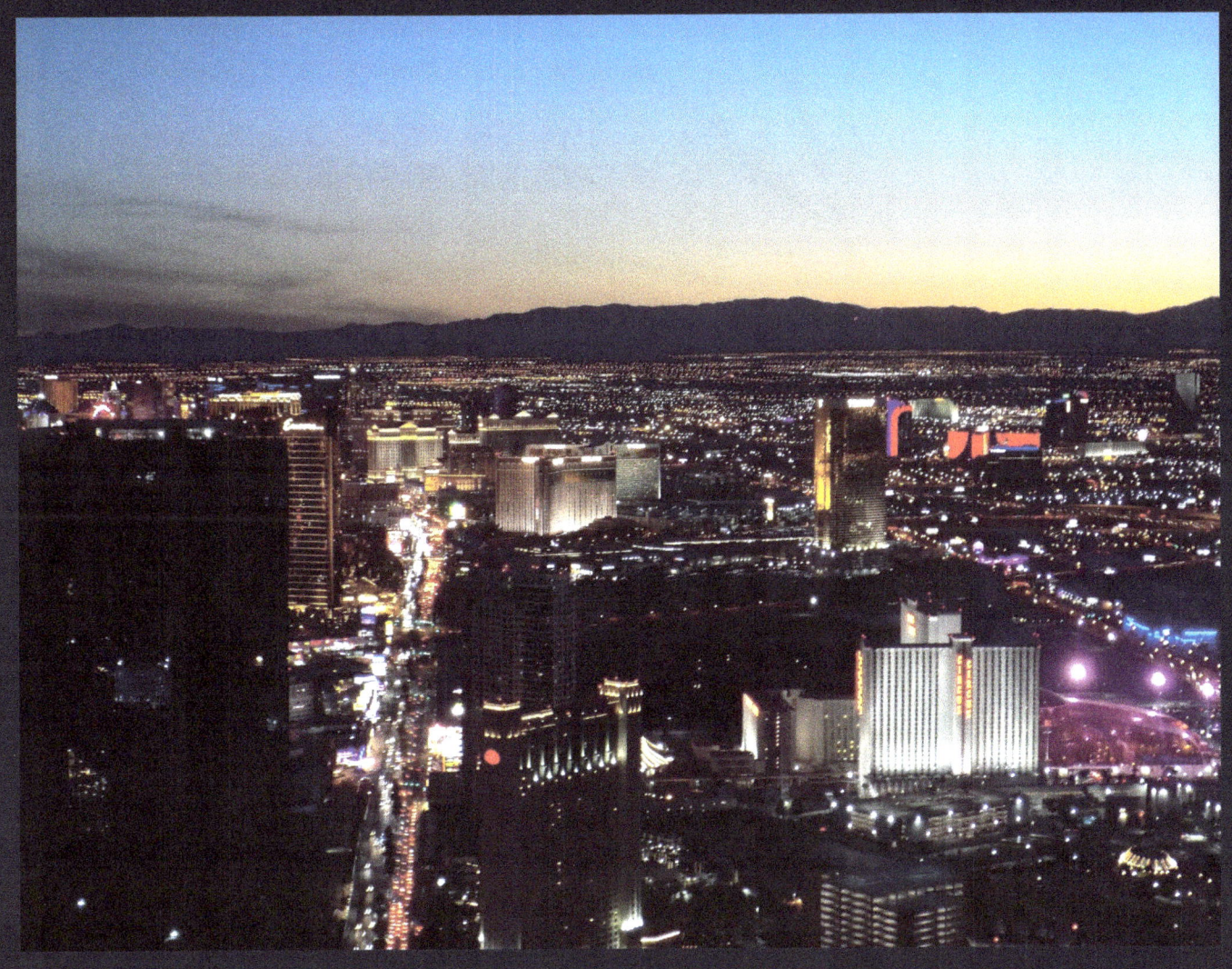

Ah, Las Vegas...it's so beautiful with all its hustle bustle along the Strip and bright lights. Well, except for that big dark monolith on the far left side of this picture where the Fontainebleau sits dark and desolate.

But perhaps you'll notice another gaping black hole amidst the city lights in this shot? Take a look near the center of this photo, across the Strip from the Fontainebleau, just above Circus Circus Hotel & Casino and below the Trump Tower. Enter the failed Echelon Hotel & Casino, also hiding in plain sight.

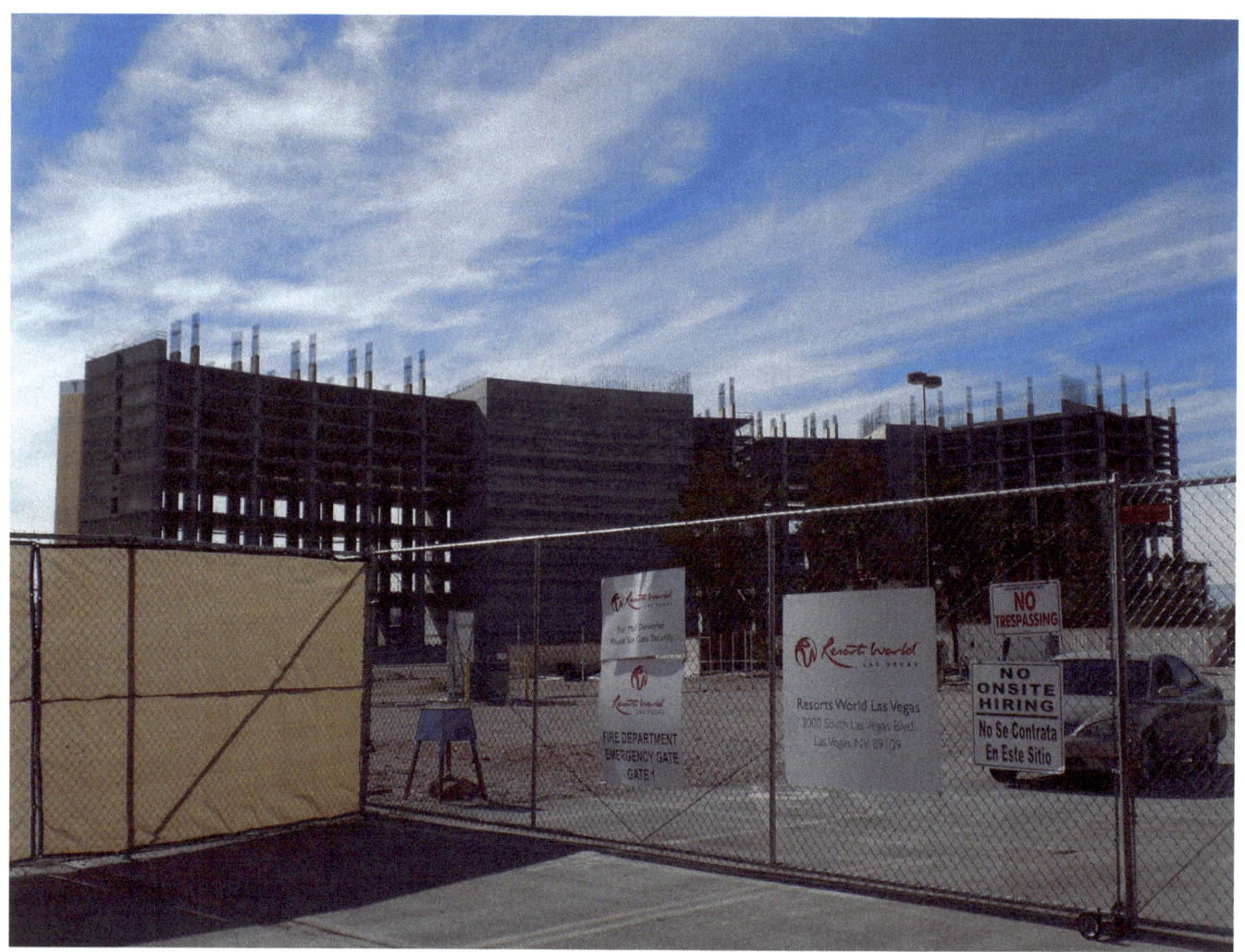

Former site of the Stardust Hotel & Casino, the 87-acre parcel located at the northwest corner of the Las Vegas Blvd. and Desert Inn Rd. intersection was to become home to the Echelon Hotel & Casino. Construction on the $4.8 billion Boyd Gaming site began in 2007 but then halted in 2008, and the property has since sat inactive for the past seven years.

Echelon was originally supposed to open in 2010 with nearly 5,000 rooms spread over five hotels and was to feature a casino, convention space and theaters. During the Recession, Boyd Gaming ran into roadblocks while trying to obtain additional financing, and the project halted.

The Stardust, which opened in 1958, had a 48-year run on the turf but closed in November 2006 and was imploded on March 13, 2007, to make way for the Echelon. The Stardust met its demise a year prior to the market crash and onset of the Recession. In retrospect, assuming Stardust was generating even a little revenue (had they not demolished the casino), it likely would've generated more income for Boyd over these past 8 years than what the incomplete steel skeleton of the would-be Echelon has coughed up.

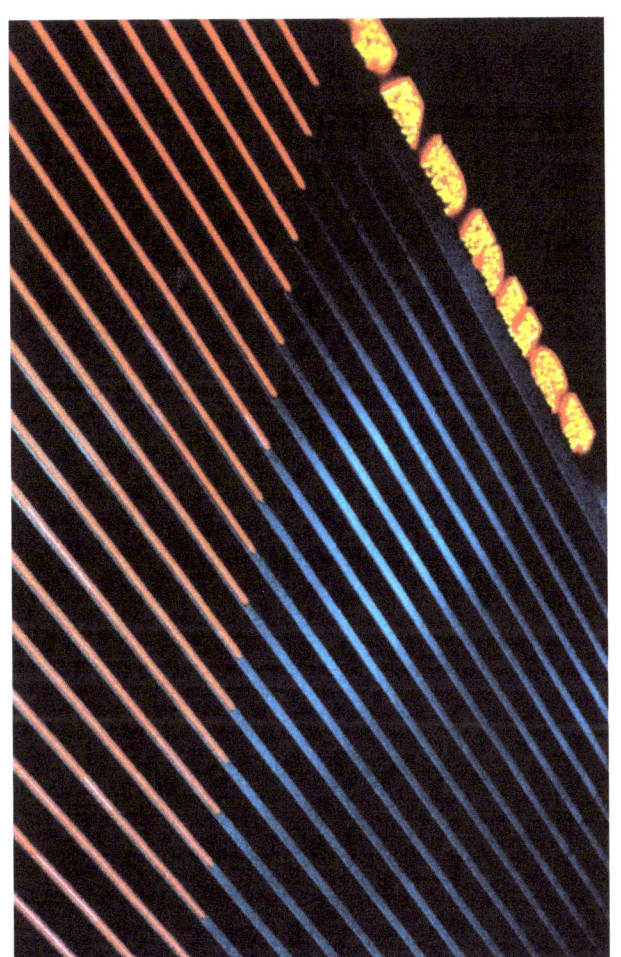

But there is finally hope for this long-since inactive site. In March 2013, Boyd Gaming sold it for $350 million to the Genting Group. On May 5, 2015, Malaysia-based Genting Berhad broke ground on the new $4 billion Asian-themed complex Resorts World Las Vegas. Set to include a replica of the Great Wall of China, a live panda bear habitat, a 7.5 acre indoor water park and tea gardens, it is expected to take several years before the facility is open to the public. The property will include a 3,000-room hotel, 30 food and beverage outlets and a 4,000-seat theater.

Considering Stardust closed in 2006, even if Resorts World opened next year in 2016 (of course, improbable), this land joins the Fontainebleau in the not-so-esteemed club of properties that haven't seen any consumer activity in over a decade.

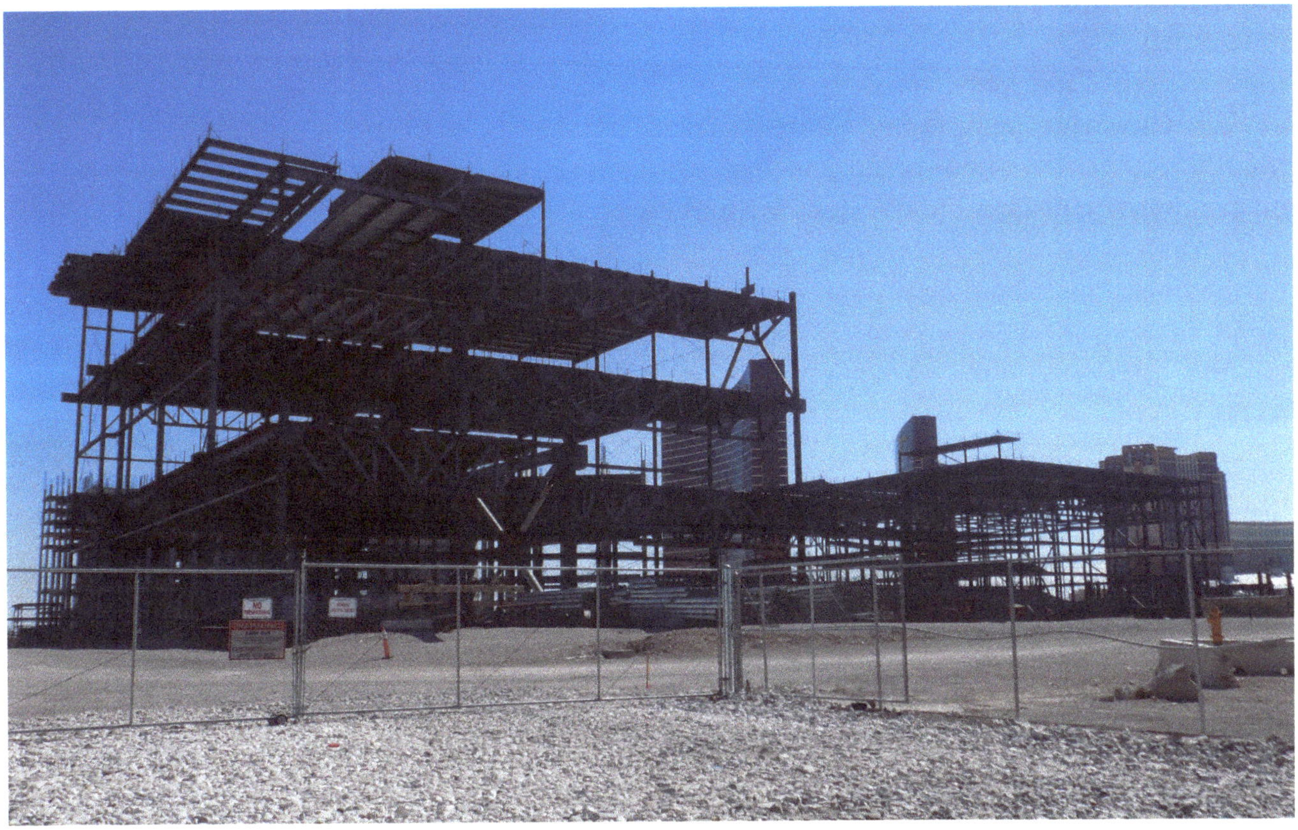

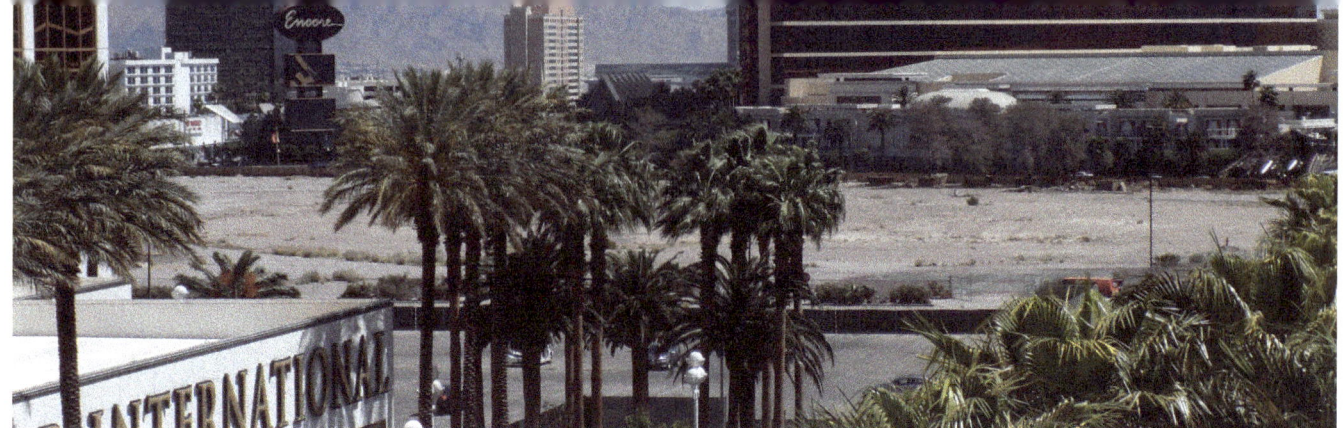

And just next door to the former site of the Stardust/Echelon sits another property (pictured above, the empty lot across from the Wynn and Encore resorts/casinos and adjacent to Trump International) that will also likely join the dormant-for-a-decade club.

Former home to the New Frontier Hotel & Casino, the 36-acre site located at the northwest corner of the Las Vegas Blvd. and Fashion Show Dr. intersection has sat inactive since July 2007, when the New Frontier closed its doors after roughly a 65-year run. The New Frontier was imploded on November 13, 2007, just a few short months after its closure.

In May 2007, Israeli company the Elad Group acquired the New Frontier from previous owner, real estate and casino mogul Phil Ruffin, for more than $1.24 billion. At the time, it was considered one of the most expensive real estate deals of all time on the Strip. When Elad ran into financing issues to develop out its planned $5 billion hotel-casino based on the Plaza Hotel in New York City, the project stalled. In August 2014, Crown Resorts paid $260 million to acquire a controlling stake in the parcel.

To date, Crown has plans to begin construction of a hotel-casino project sometime this year. As of May 2015, when the above photo was shot, there are still tumbleweeds blowing around in the wind on this property. Fingers crossed for the future.

On the backside of the property formerly home to the New Frontier, now sits the Trump International Hotel. Trump owns a 50 percent interest in the 64-story luxury hotel/condos/timeshare building that features exterior windows gilded in 24-carat gold. Trump developed the property alongside Phil Ruffin.

But even Donald Trump wasn't immune to the Recession. Trump's original plans called for two identical towers on the parcel, but when the Recession set in, financiers pulled out, halting Trump's plans. His first (and only) tower opened March 31, 2008, just weeks after the collapse of investment bank Bear Stearns, shortly prior to the Wall Street meltdown. Bad timing, indeed, and no tower number two for Trump.

To date, the lots for Trump's second tower that never was, as well as the lot that served as home to the New Frontier, still remain vacant.

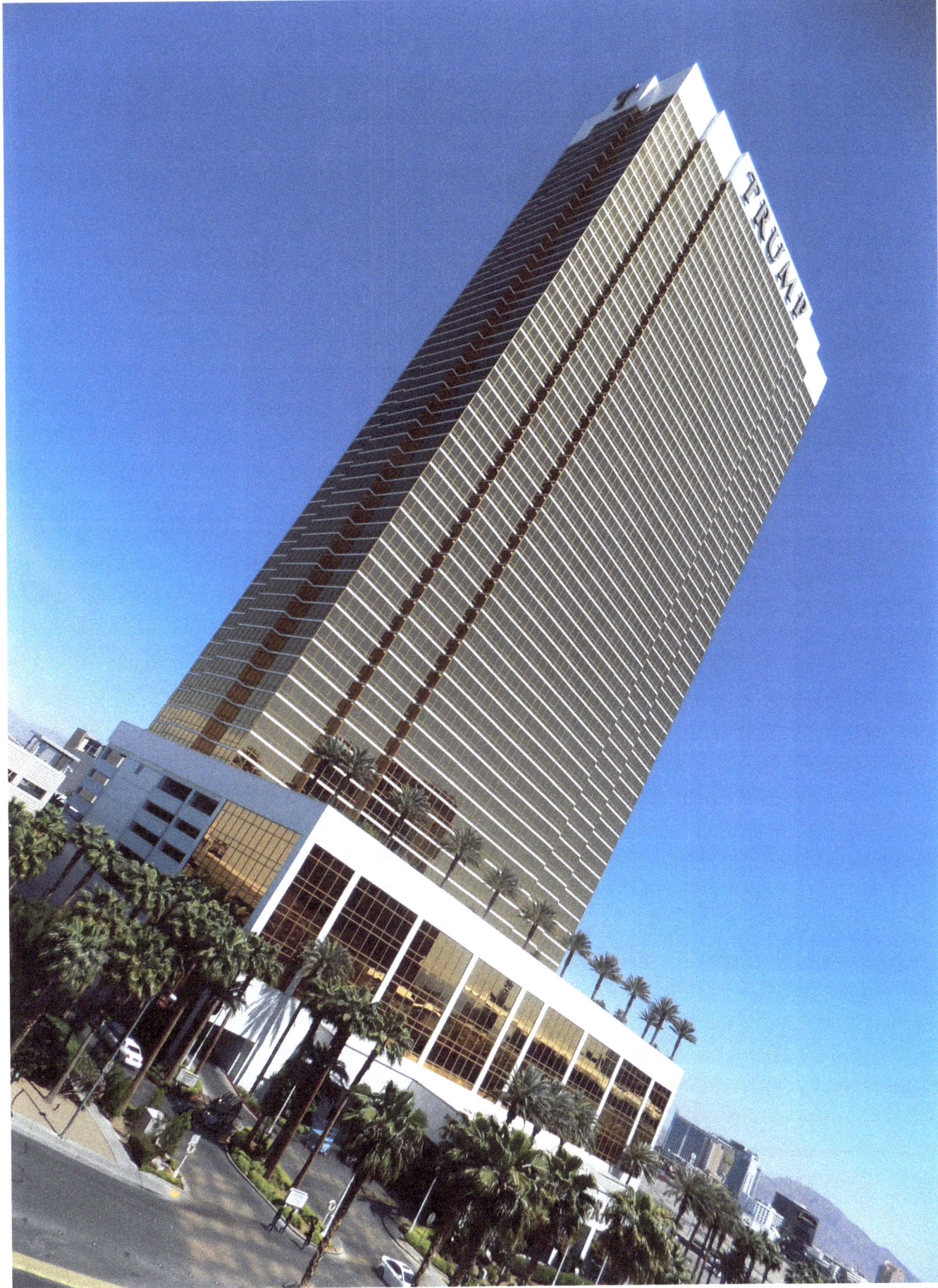

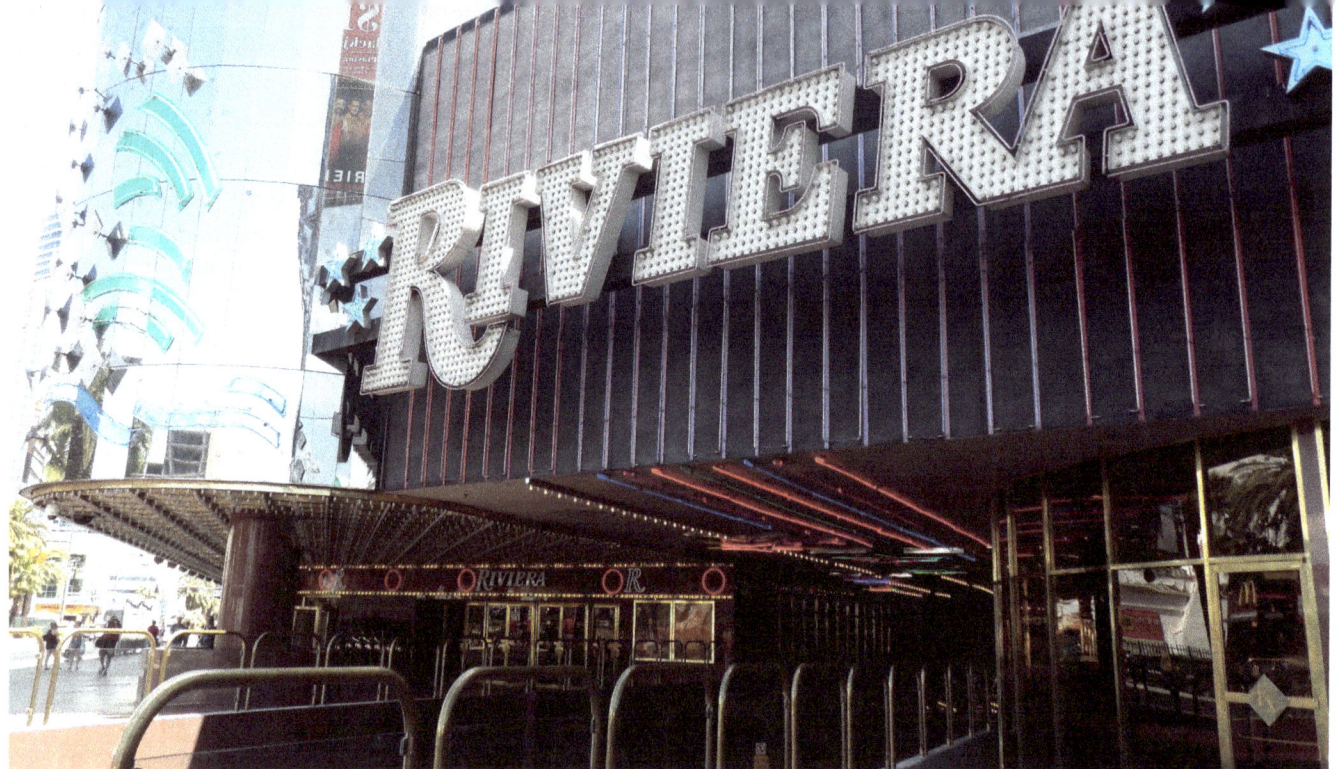

On May 4, 2015, the Riviera Hotel & Casino was the latest in a long line of vintage Strip stalwarts to close its doors. The property was purchased by the Las Vegas Convention and Visitors Authority for just under $191 million. Currently located behind the casino on Paradise Road, the LVCVA plans to develop out the Strip-front property over the next 5-7 years.

LVCVA's $2.3 billion Las Vegas Global Business District will give the Convention Center a Strip-front address and include a major expansion of the Las Vegas Convention Center with new and upgraded facilities, a trade center and a multimodal transportation hub.

For fans of the casino's infamous Crazy Girls statue, which sat just outside the front doors, there's good news. On closing day, the statue was carted off at noon (pictured right) to its new home at the Planet Hollywood Hotel & Casino. At the same time, the pool had been shut down, and the property was already being fenced off, as guests and curious onlookers were politely ushered out of the casino for the last time. When asked regarding what date the casino would be imploded, two different staff members report that while it's tentatively scheduled for the fall, it likely won't happen until 2016.

The Riviera is the latest closure in a line of classic casinos hit by the Recession: The New Frontier (currently an empty lot next to the Trump International Hotel), the Stardust (currently the stalled Echelon project set to be Resorts World), the Sahara (now the glittery and bustling SLS Hotel & Casino) and Imperial Palace (now occupied by The Linq Hotel & Casino and must-see High Roller observation wheel). Riviera's neighbor, the defunct Fontainebleau, is reflected in the mirrored side of the building (pictured opposite page, lower right).

Just weeks prior to its closing, the Riviera had celebrated its 60th anniversary on April 20, 2015.

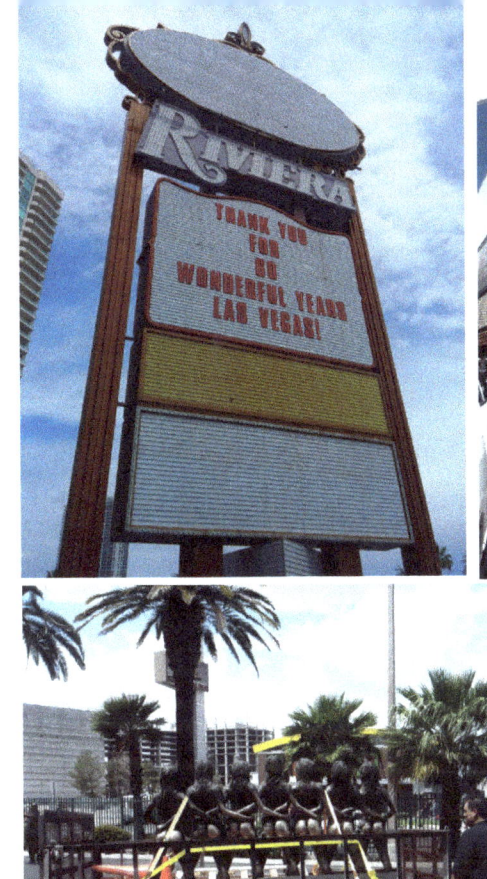
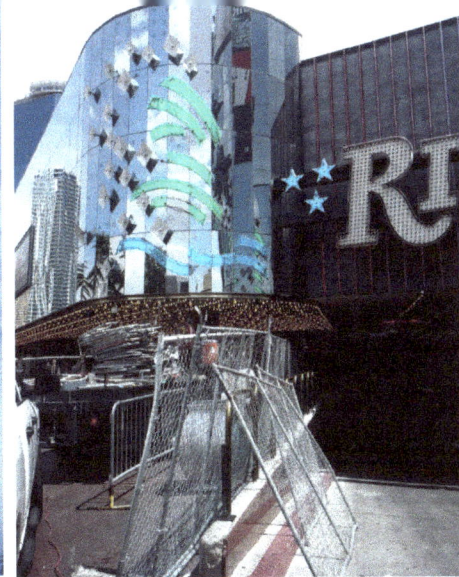
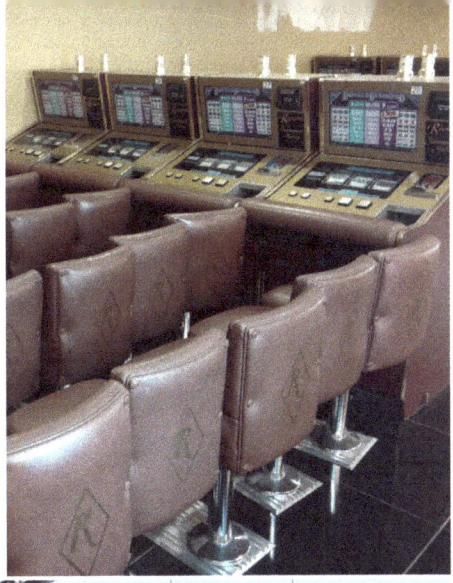
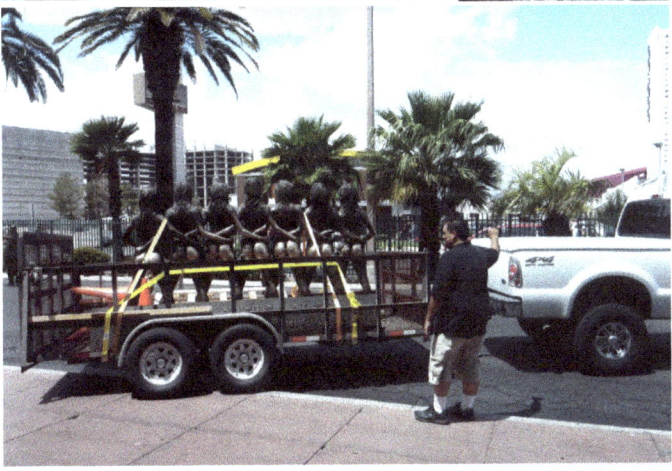
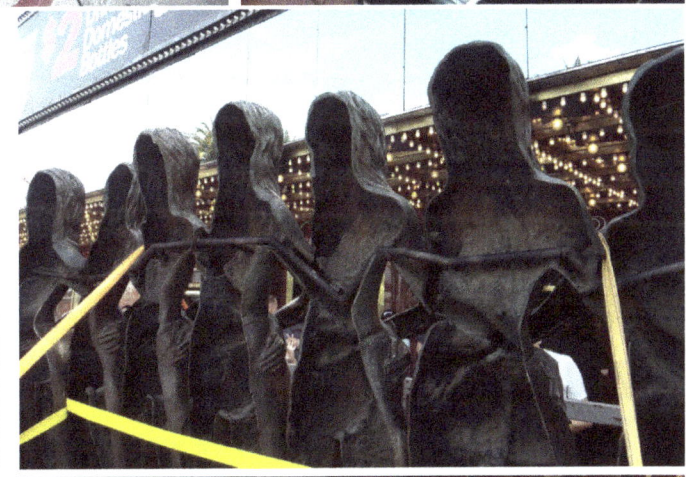
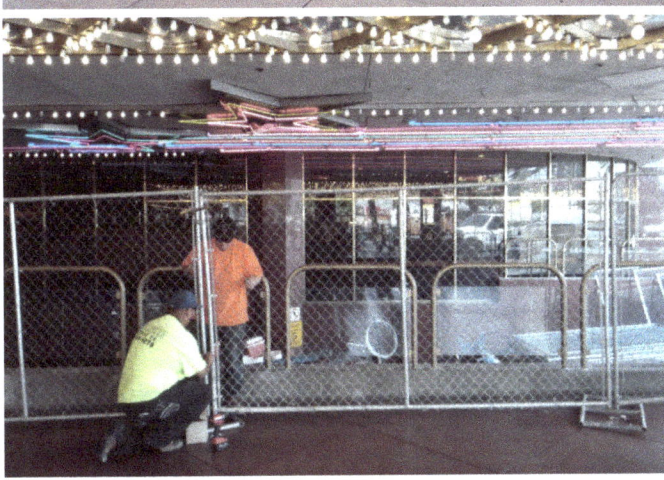
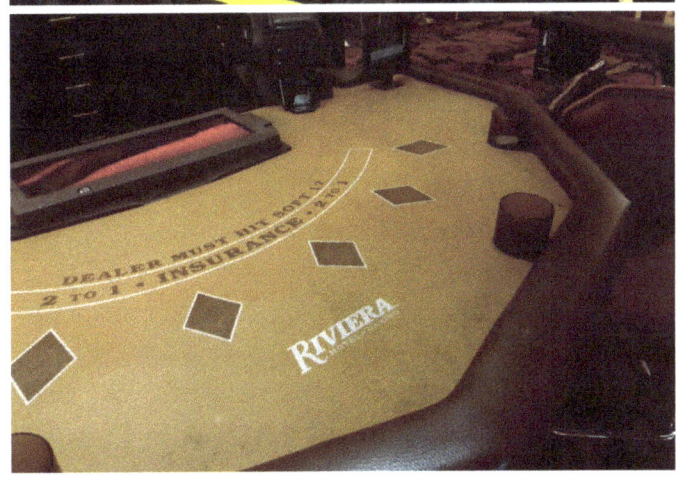
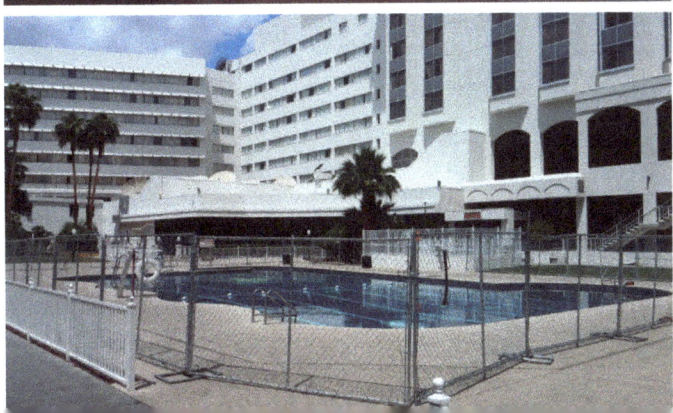
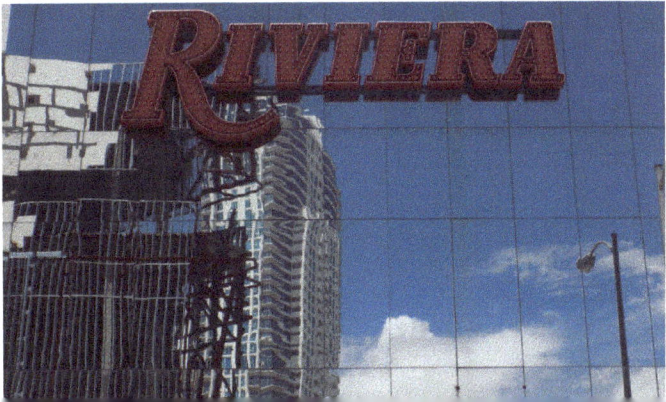

Heading further south towards center Strip, one of Vegas' biggest blunders sits front and center for all to see - but you'll have to look closely, as it's hiding under a big black tarp (pictured, right).

The Harmon Tower, at Harmon Ave. and Las Vegas Blvd., is part of the massive CityCenter complex (which includes the Aria, Vdara and Mandarin Oriental towers) and was to be a 49-floor hotel and condominium tower budgeted at $8.5-billion.

In 2008 (a year before CityCenter's opening), city inspectors halted construction at the 26th floor because of faulty steel reinforcement columns, citing the building would crumble if a strong earthquake hit. While Vegas is susceptible to smaller tremors, it rarely sees quakes with the magnitude required to bring the building down. But better safe than sorry. As of May 2015, the Harmon Tower is still in the deconstruction process.

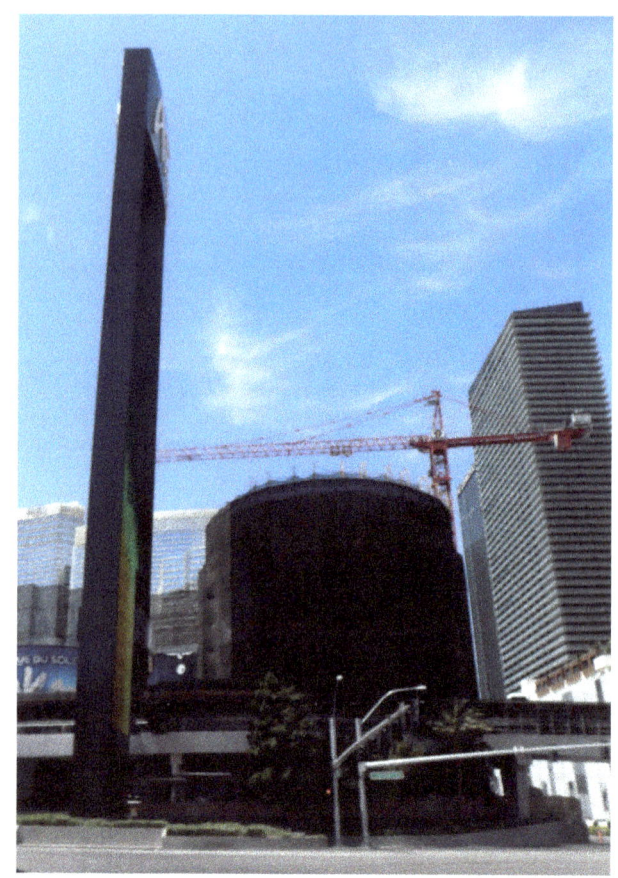

And heading to the southernmost part of the Strip, all that remains of the Skyvue Las Vegas Super Wheel are two massive concrete towers (opposite page), which have been sitting inactive since March 2013. Located directly across from the Mandalay Bay Hotel & Casino, the SkyVue was intended to be a 500-ft. tall ferris wheel. Plagued by money troubles and numerous delays in construction, Skyvue developer Howard Bulloch has already endured at least eight lawsuits filed by the project's various contractors.

With the opening of the High Roller (pictured, right) on March 31, 2014, the Strip gained the world's tallest ferris wheel, topping out at 550 feet. The centerpiece of Caesars Entertainment Corporation's $550 million the LINQ complex, High Roller has become a popular destination spot, which begs the question, "Does the Strip really need two super-sized ferris wheels?" As of May 2015, the future remains unclear for SkyVue.

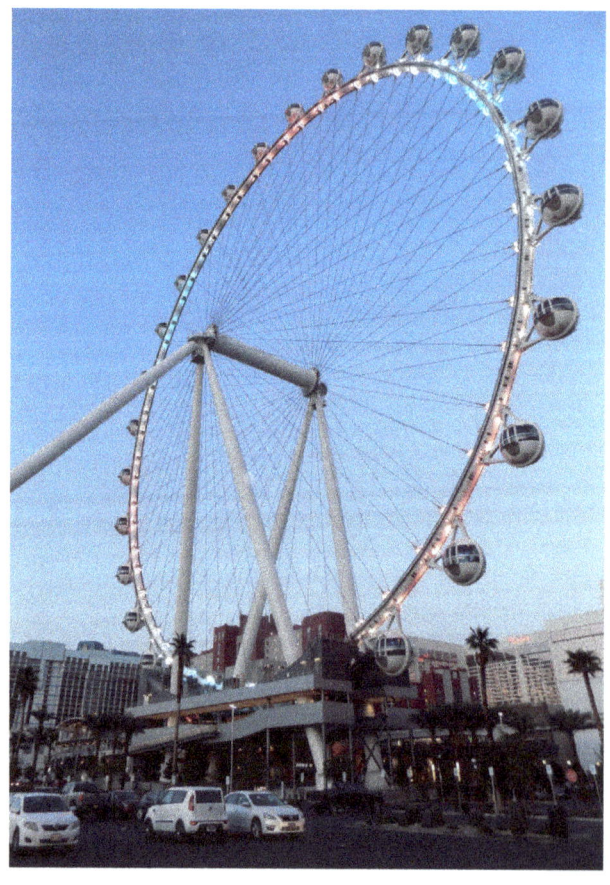

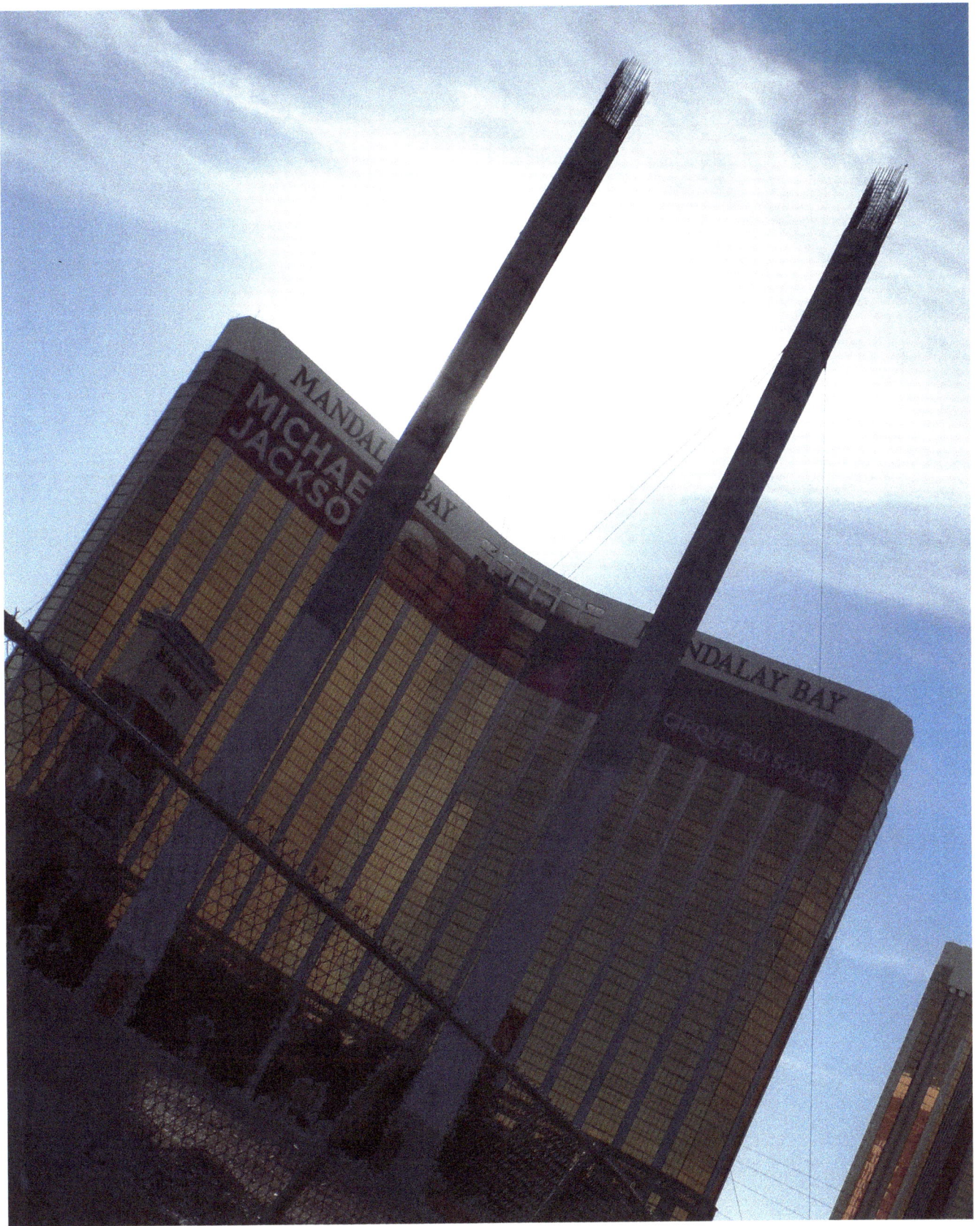

# checking out?

Tourism and the hospitality industry are two of the city's biggest moneymakers. In the '90s, it was common to get a night at a decent hotel on the Strip with a coupon for an all-you-can-eat buffet for under $20. But at the onset of Vegas' boom days, things changed, and prices went up. Along with the price increase, however, came many new options, as casinos were constantly building bigger and better to capture the hearts, minds and wallets of tourists. In the aftermath of the crash, many of the big resorts are still struggling, so imagine what that means for smaller, older hotels.

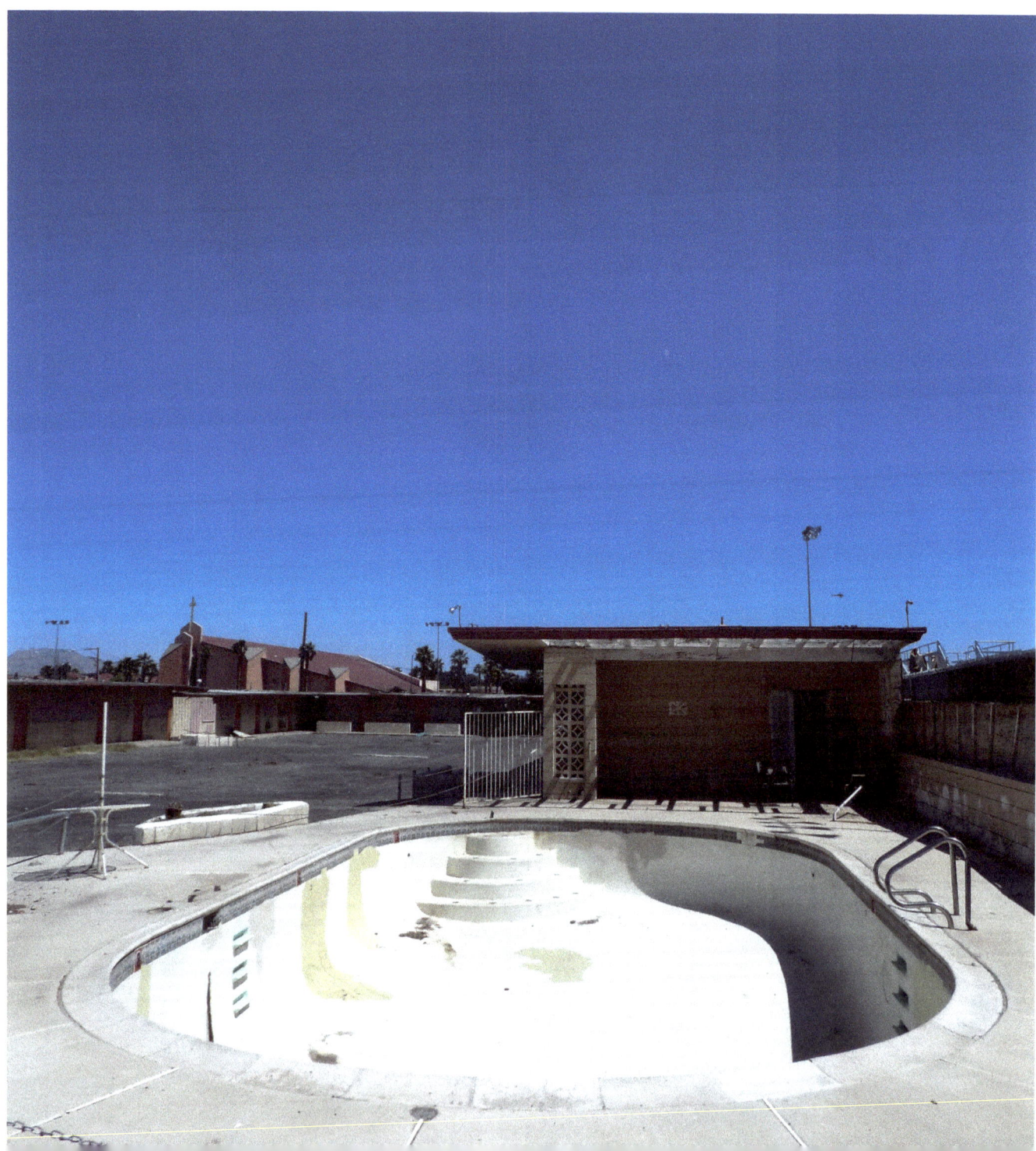

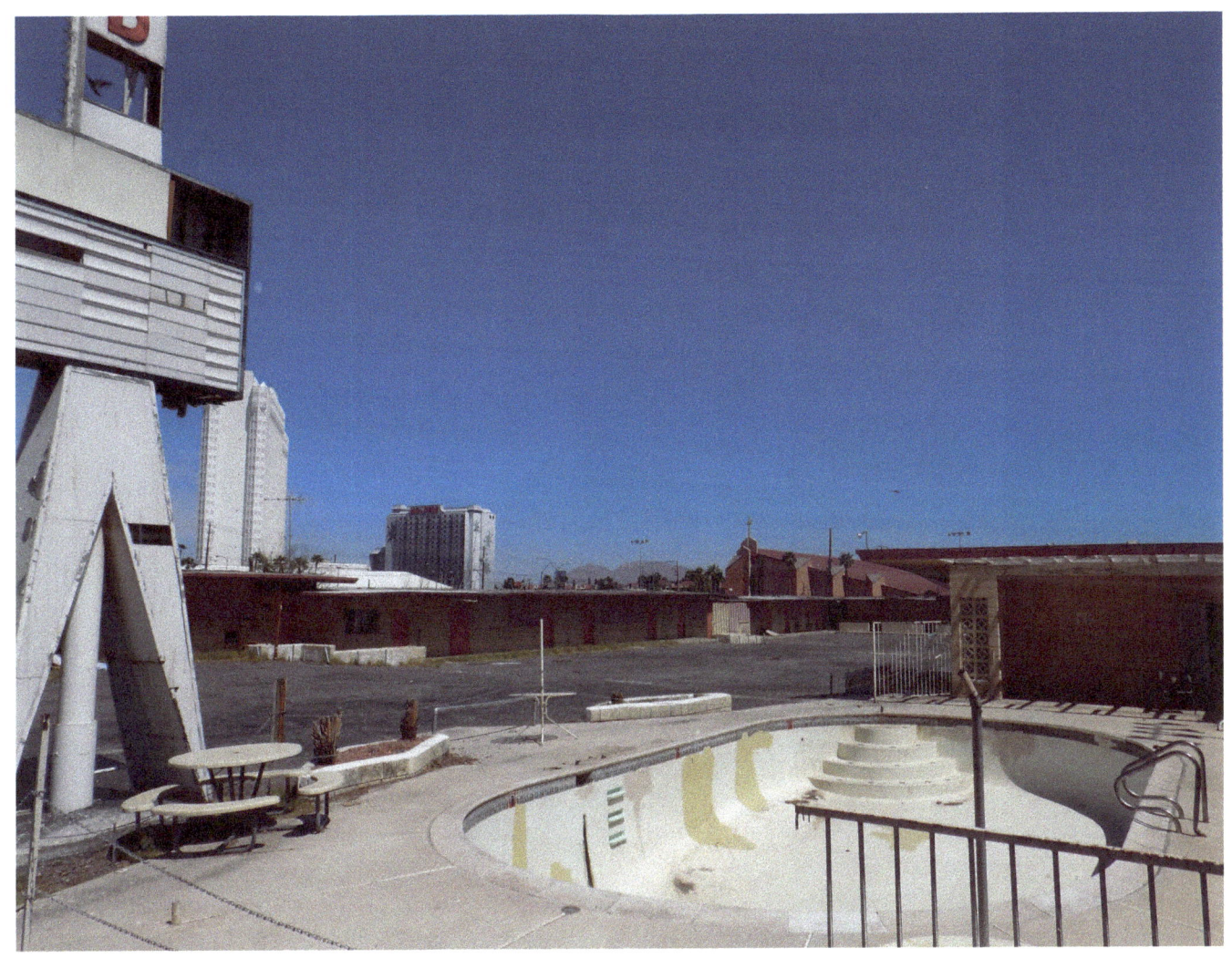

Built in 1959, the White Sands Motel sits boarded up on the south side of the Strip, facing the gleaming Luxor Hotel & Casino. The property was closed for business by 2000, long before the Recession hit, but the motel sits along a massive stretch of the undeveloped South Strip, which was affected by the Recession.

Much of the land across from the Mandalay Bay and Luxor had been purchased during the boom years with big plans for new resorts and casinos, which ended up folding during the Recession. In 2001, plans for World Port Resorts, a London-themed project with a casino, hotel, fine-arts facility and convention center, were announced - yet despite much of the land being cleared, the project never came to be. And all that remains of these failed business ventures are massive, vacant stretches of land and forgotten properties, including the White Sands.

The White Sands Motel is now home to an out-of-control feral cat colony.

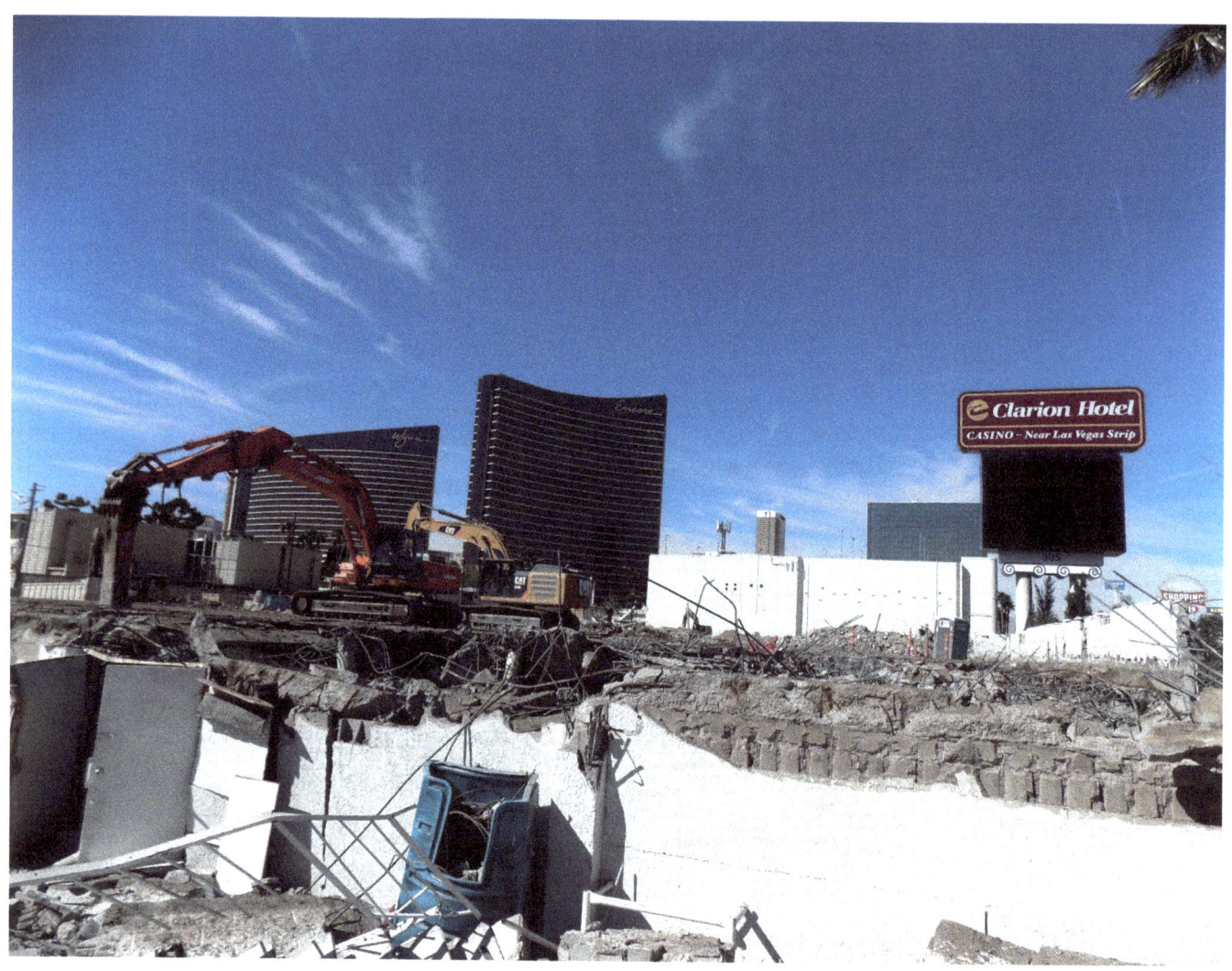

The off-Strip Clarion Hotel, which was located on Convention Center Dr. just west of the Las Vegas Convention Center, closed Sept. 2, 2014, and was imploded Feb. 10, 2015. Opened in 1970 as a Royal Inn, the hotel saw numerous reincarnations, becoming the Royal Americana Hotel, Paddlewheel Hotel Casino and then Debbie Reynolds' Hollywood Hotel when the star purchased the property in 1992.

After Reynolds sold the property in 1999, it was owned for a short time by the World Wrestling Federation, and was then sold and remodeled as the Greek Isles Hotel & Casino. In 2007, real-estate developer DI Development Group purchased the property with big plans to turn it into a mixed-use space with a bigger hotel, convention area, restaurants and shops. But as the Recession set in, that didn't happen, and the property went into bankruptcy in 2009.

It eventually became the Clarion in April 2013, just a little over a year before the property finally closed for good. Since its implosion, the land has been completely cleared, and all that remains is is the hotel sign.

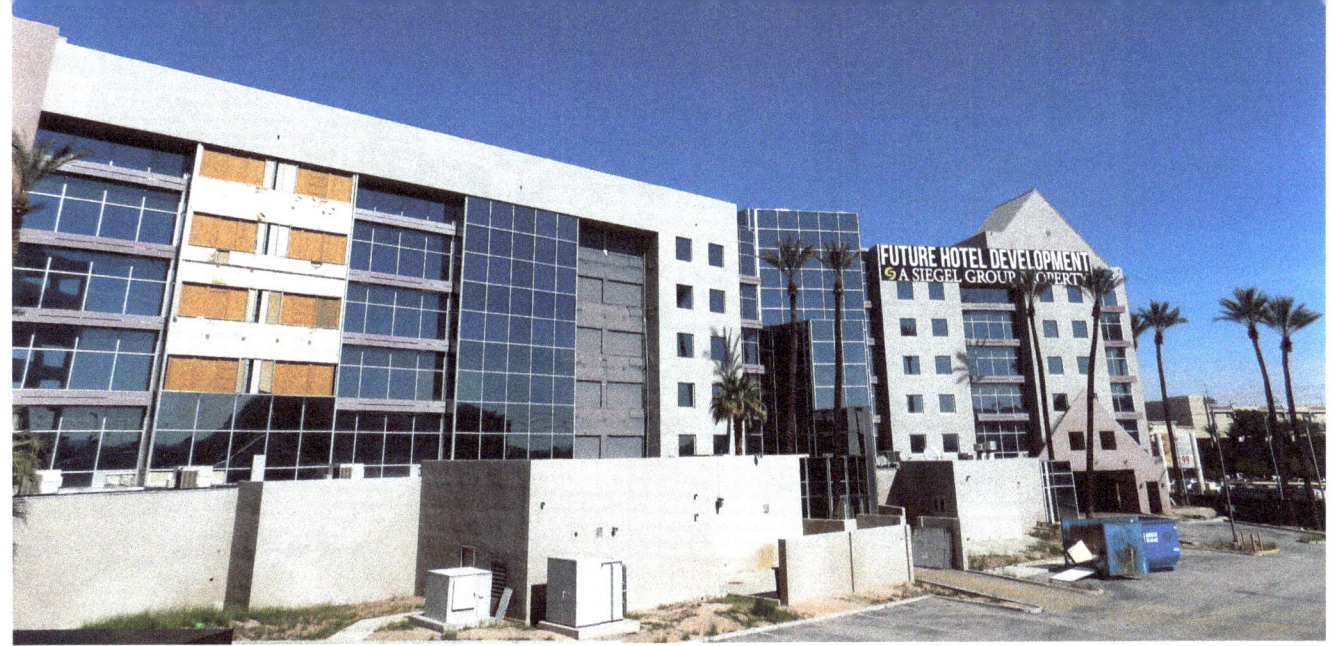

Formerly the Atrium Suites Hotel, this six-story property at 4255 Paradise Road is located right next door to the Hard Rock Hotel and is only a few short blocks to McCarran International Airport.

Now owned by the Siegel Group, the property, which sits on approximately 3.75 acres of land, has exchanged hands a few times in recent years - eventually going for bargain-basement prices. A/P Hotel LLC paid $50.5 million for it in Sept. 2007. (Prior to Atrium Suites' occupation, it had been a Holiday Inn Crown Plaza.) In July 2011, LV Opportunity Fund nabbed it for only $2 million - wow! That's quite a drop in price. By the time Siegel Group came in and bought in December 2011, they still landed a relative bargain, purchasing the property for $4.2 mil.

Siegel initially planned to partner with a national hotel brand to reopen the facility within a year, yet as of mid-2015, the property still sits vacant.

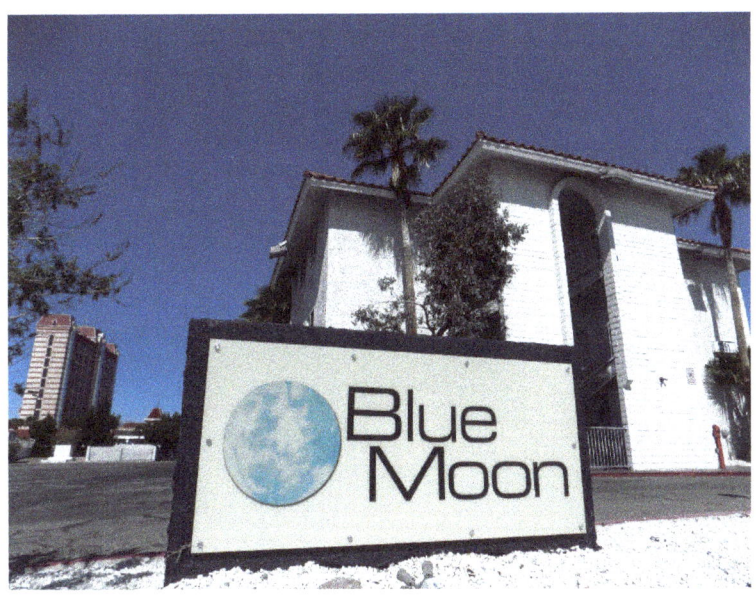

After a 12-year run, the Blue Moon Resort closed its doors on October 15, 2014. The gay community mainstay was located on Westwood Dr., just east of the I-15 and south of Sahara Blvd. in a primarily industrial area.

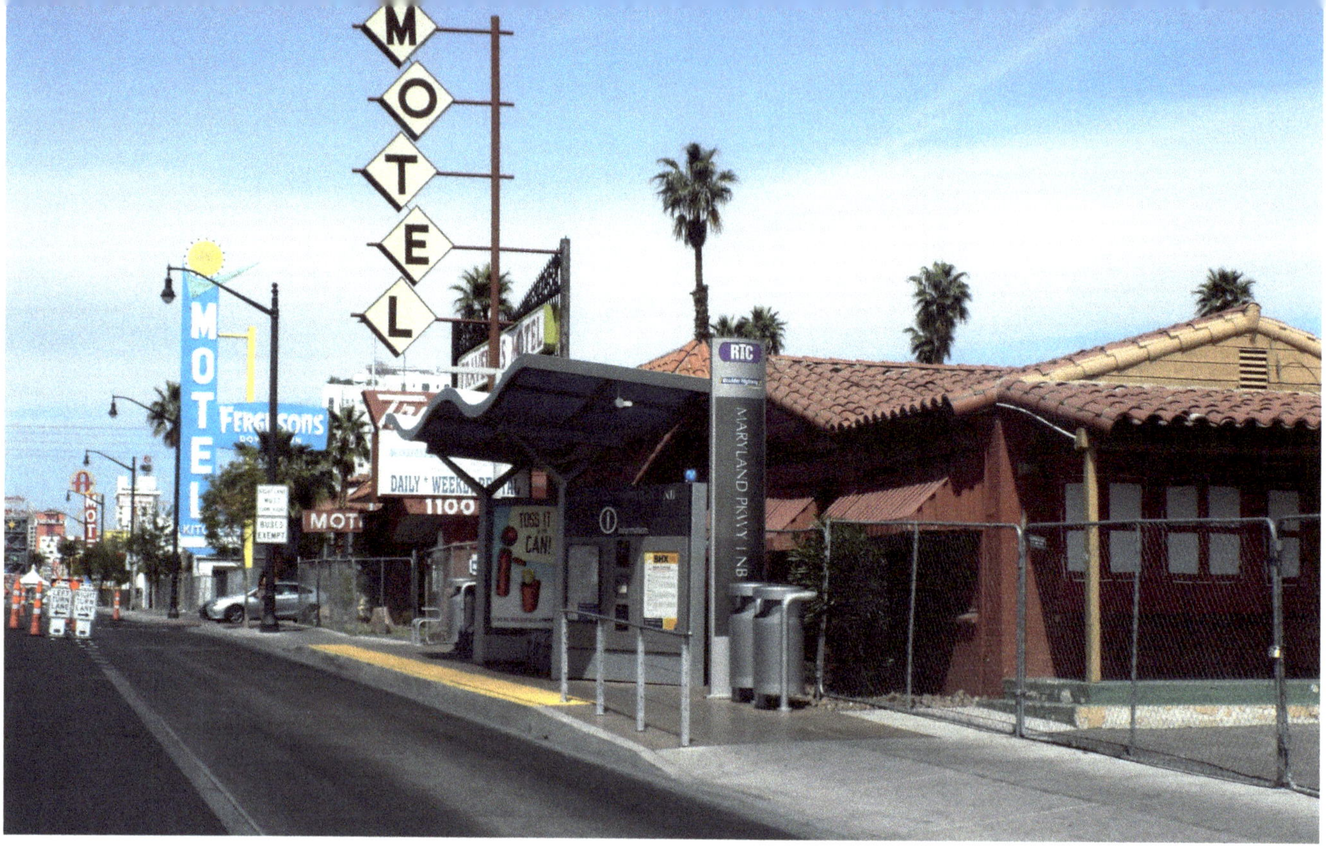

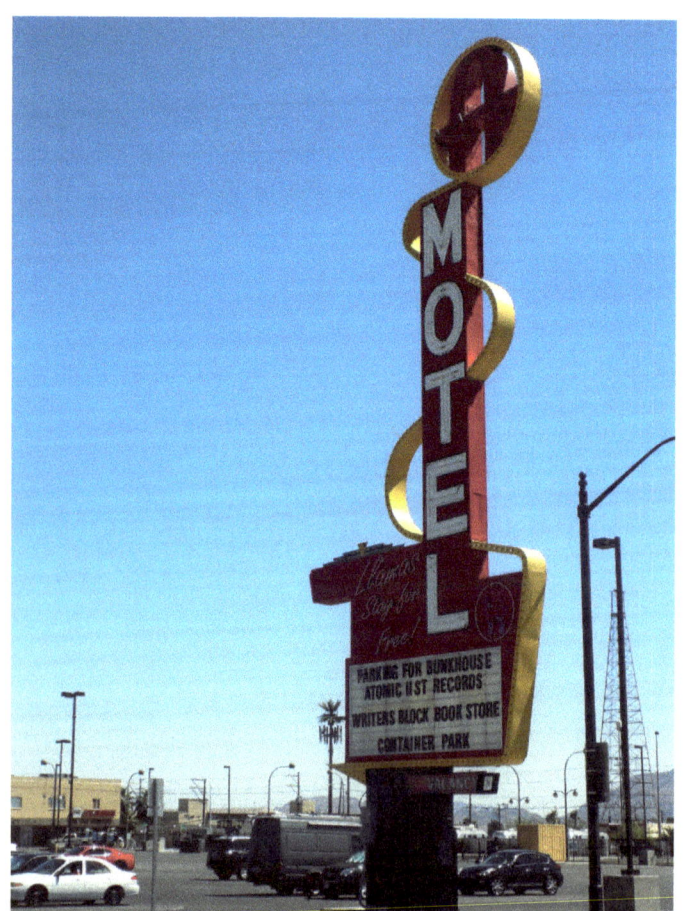

The demise of Vegas' past is most evident on a two- to three-mile stretch of Fremont St. that runs from Las Vegas Blvd. at the west to Eastern Blvd. at the east. This section of Fremont St. is littered with vacant motels from days past that are currently boarded up or fenced off.

At the far west side of this stretch, just a few blocks from the gates of the newly rehabbed Fremont St. Experience, sits this A Motel sign. It's all that remains from the Ambassador Motel, which opened in 1952 and closed in 1996. It remained vacant until it was demolished in 2007. Currently, the site is used for parking.

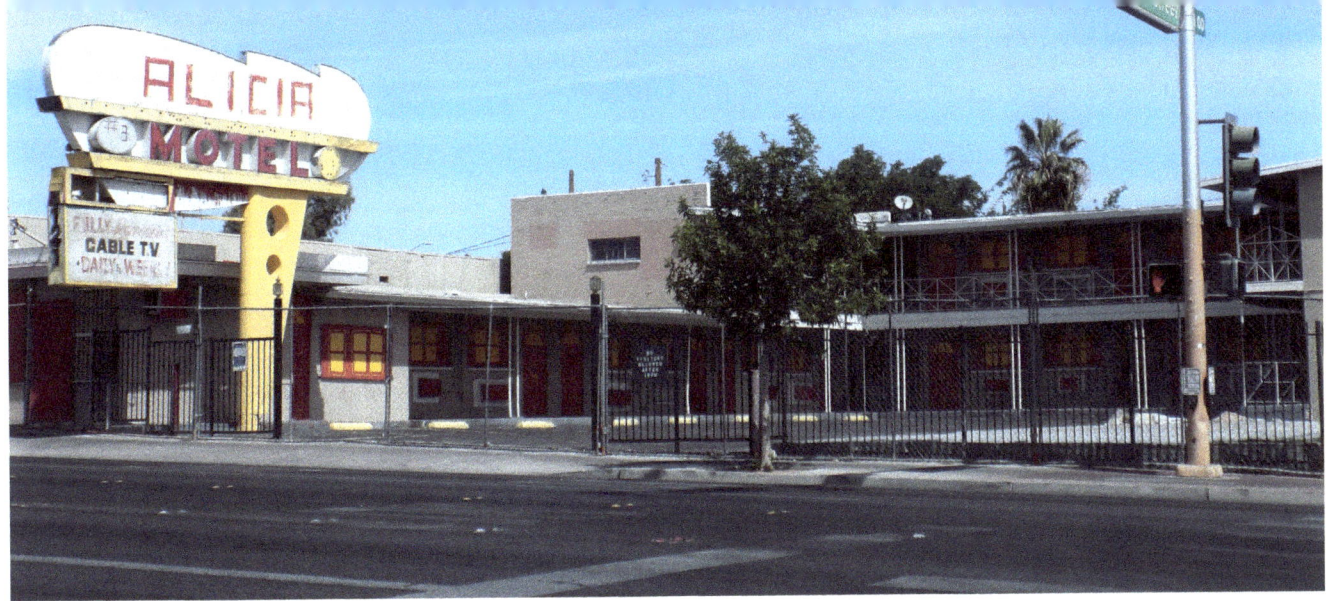

Just east of the former Ambassador, at Fremont St. and 13th St., lays the remains of the Alicia Motel. Once a haven for drug dealers and prostitutes alike, it is now one of a few vacant motels owned by the Downtown Project, a $350 million gentrification initiative halted by the Recession.

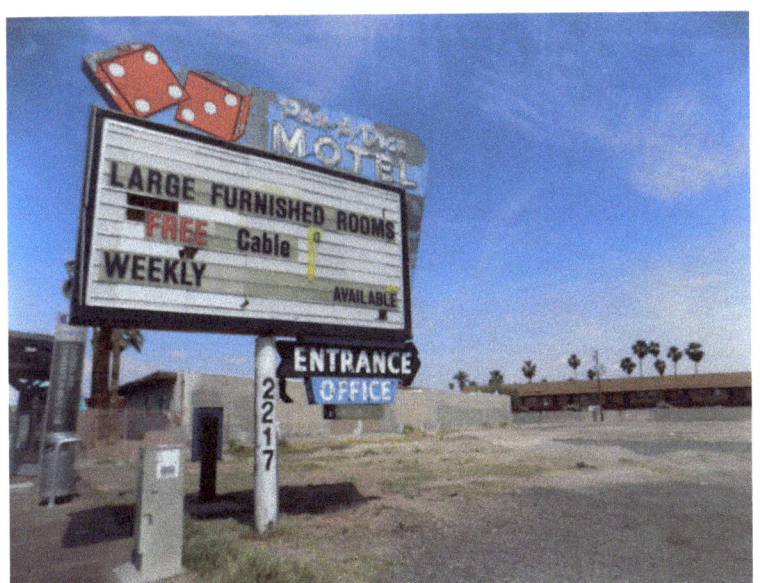

Built in 1952, the Par a Dice Motel was located on Fremont St., just west of the Charleston/ Eastern intersection and across the street from the Vegas Motel (next pages). In a state of disrepair for years, it was demolished in 2012, but its sign still remains.

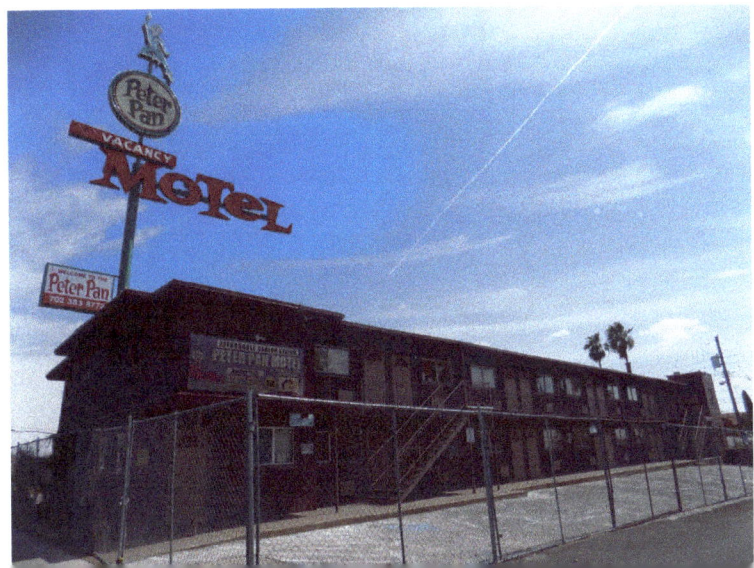

Located on 13th St. just north of Fremont St., the Peter Pan Motel was built in 1963 and finally shut its doors in 2013, when it was purchased along with neighboring residential units for $2.8 million as part of the now-stalled Fremont gentrification Downtown Project.

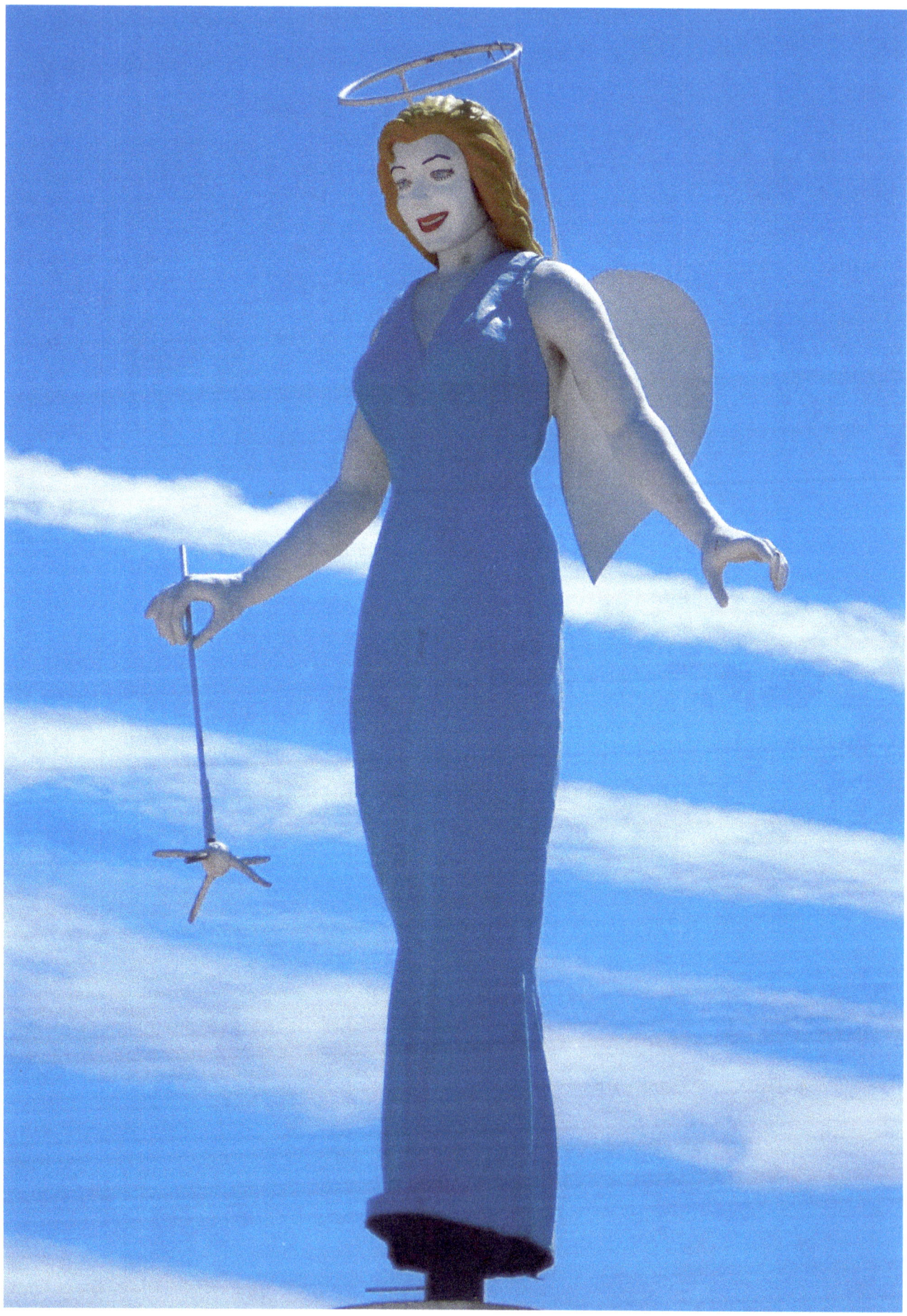

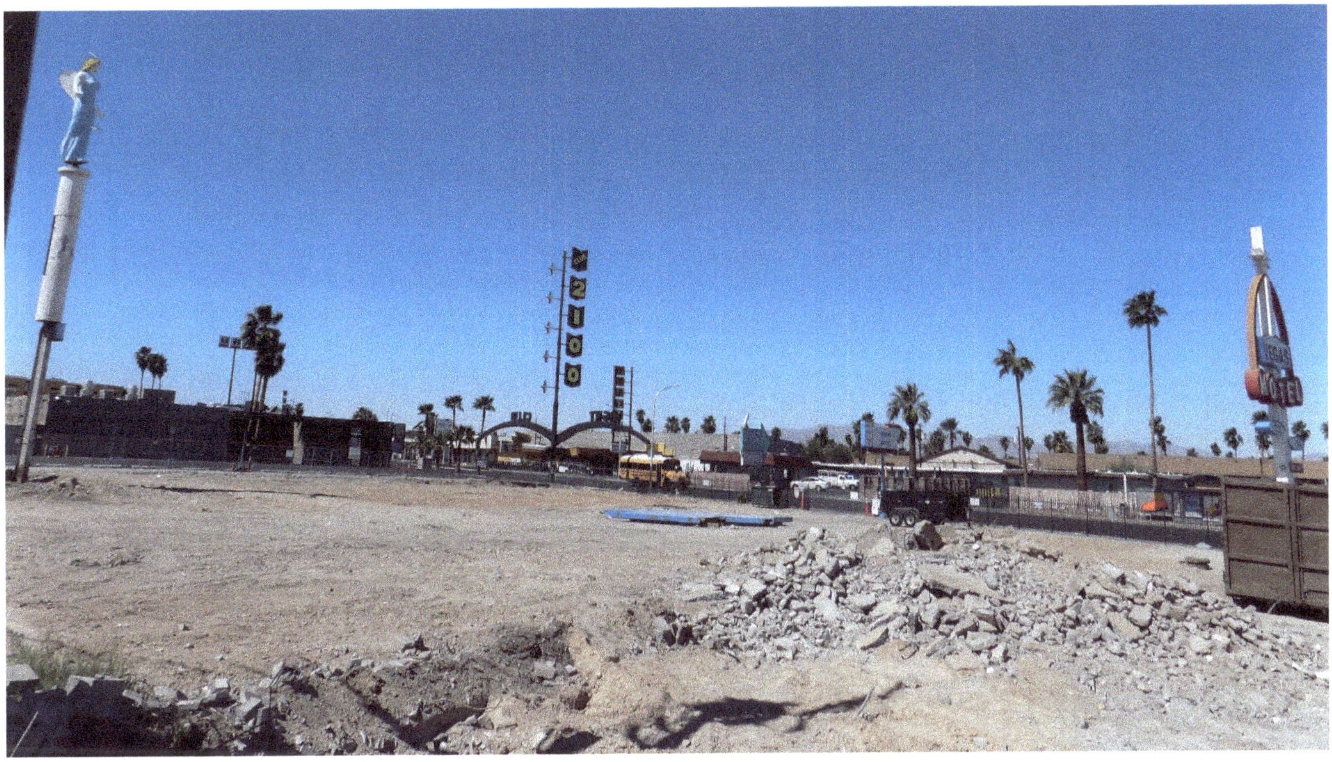

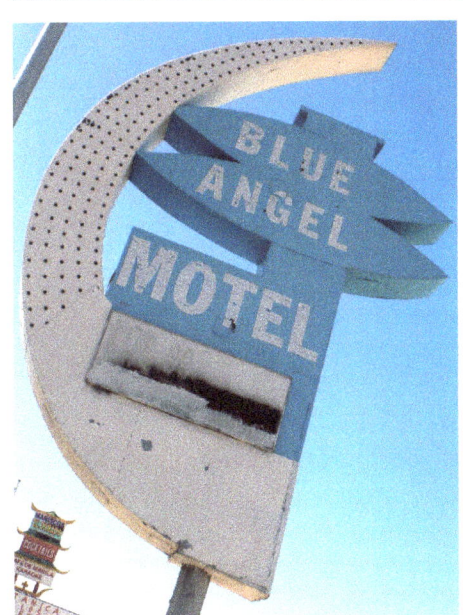

Formerly home to the Blue Angel and Vegas Motels, this massive chunk of land (just east of downtown, at the intersection of Fremont St., Eastern Ave. and Charleston Blvd.) had been purchased by developer Arnold Stalk in 2005 as part of the stalled Fremont gentrification Downtown Project. (In the photo above from March 2015, you can see what remains of the two motels after the demolition, which began in January 2015. To the far left, the iconic Blue Angel, and to the far right, the Vegas Motel sign.)

First opening its doors in 1956, the Blue Angel Motel had devolved over the decades into a seedy establishment, frequented by prostitutes and drug dealers. It closed its doors in 2011 and remained vacant until its demolition.

The motel's sign and iconic blue angel (both of which still remain) were created by neon designer Betty Willis, who also designed the Fabulous Las Vegas sign. At the time, Willis was criticized for depicting the well-endowed angel that now overlooks the pile of rubble that was once the motel. An icon for locals, the statue will be preserved. According to the property owner, she will likely end up at the Neon Museum, a graveyard for famous Vegas signs that are no longer in use.

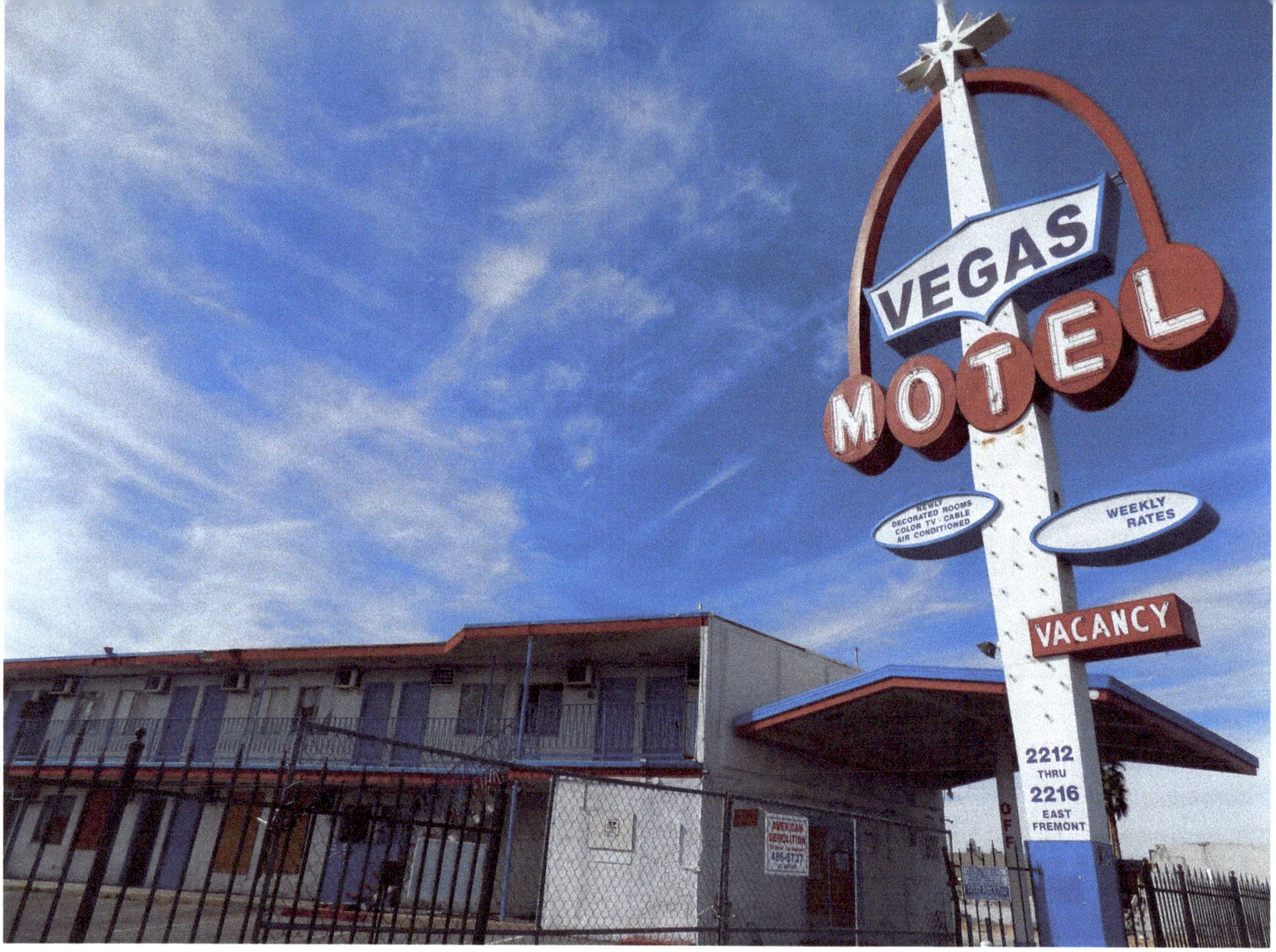

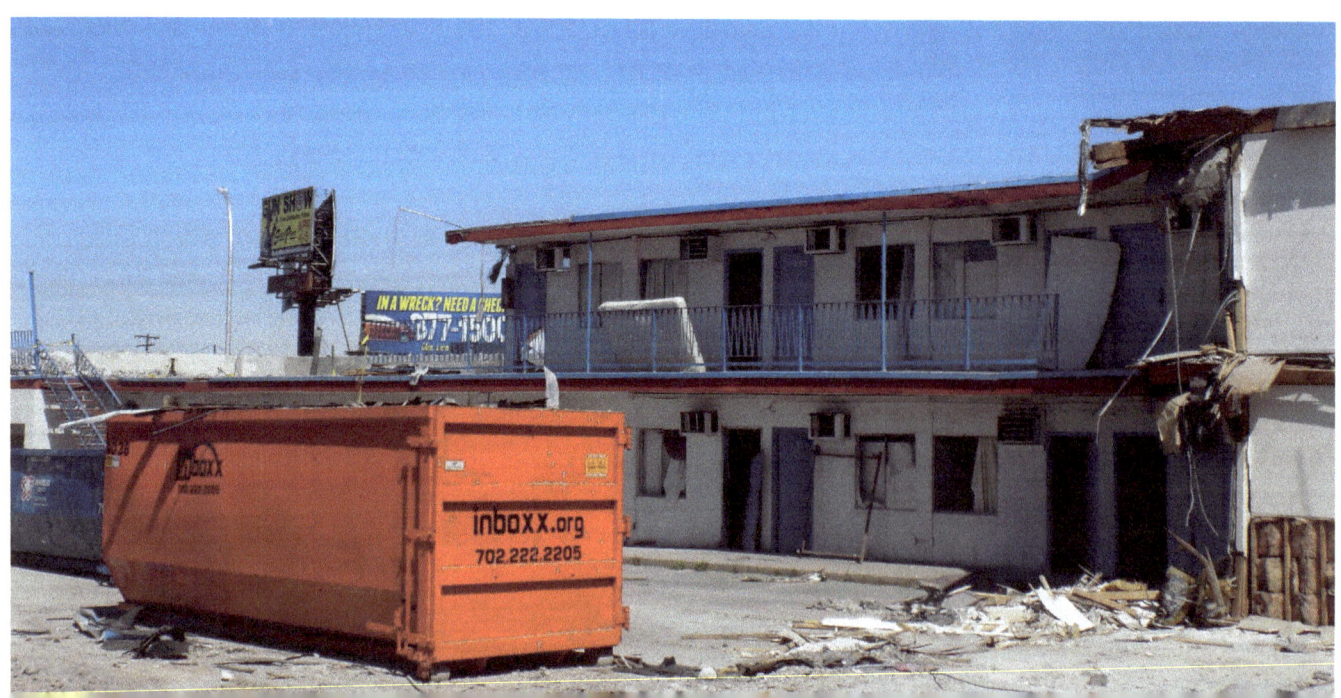

**Above:** On the Fremont St. side of the massive chunk of land that was also once home to the Blue Angel, the Vegas Motel was still standing (for the most part) as of February 2015.

**Below:** But by March, it, too, was almost entirely gone, with the exception of the sign and this small portion of the motel (which, by April, had also been razed).

# *folded*

**Above:** Not even criminals would be able to call their cell blocks home forever during the Recession. The financially troubled city of North Las Vegas closed the jail in 2012 to save the city money. Inmates were moved to the city of Las Vegas jail in an agreement that is supposed to last five years. While the city tries to come up with plans for the property, it remains vacant.

**Right:** In February 2015, RadioShack announced it would be filing for bankruptcy. As part of a major restructuring, 1,784 stores were shut down nationwide, and the rest of RadioShack's roughly 4,000 locations in the U.S. were sold to General Wireless. Pictured here at S. Maryland Pkwy. and E. Sahara Ave. is one of the 8 RadioShack locations the Las Vegas area lost.

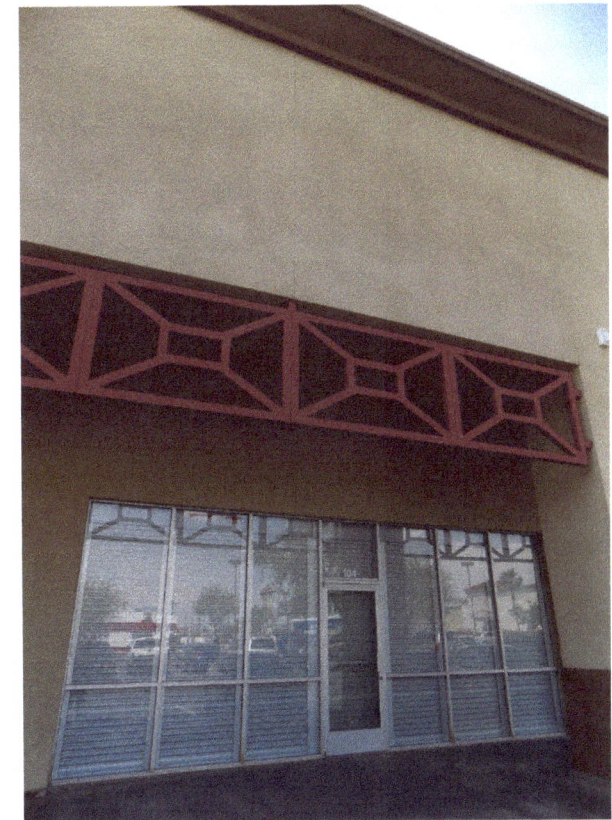

While the larger casinos have felt the burn during the Recession, many of the smaller or independent casinos have really been dealt a bad hand.

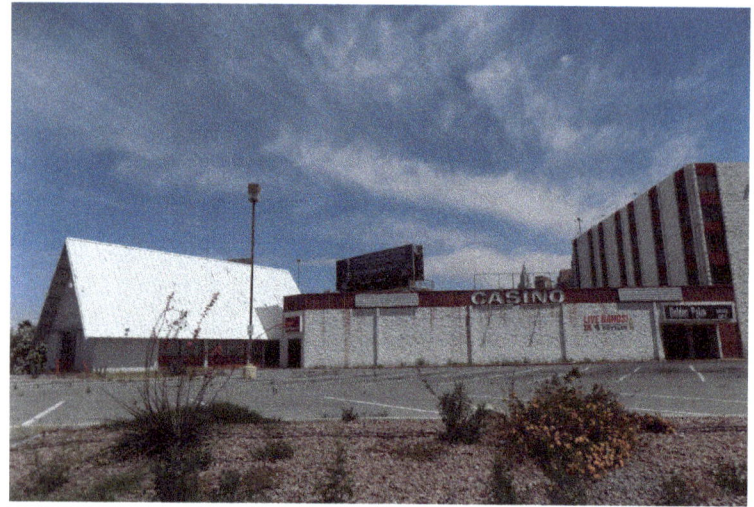

Built in 1980, the 150-room property at Tropicana Ave. and Dean Martin Dr. began as a Travelodge, became a Howard Johnson, and then in 1999 the Golden Palm Casino & Hotel when it fell under new ownership. Shut down in Feb. 2007, Recession squashed plans to make it One Trop, a 41-story hotel. Project was put on indefinite hold. Eight years later, it remains vacant.

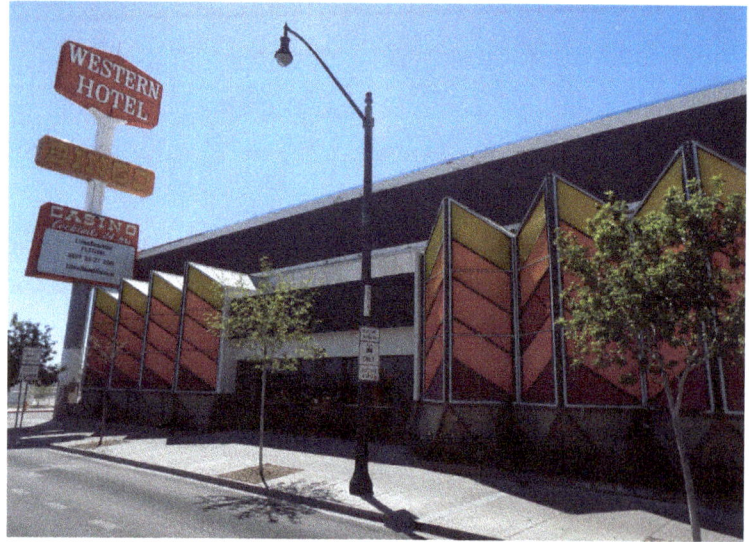

Opened in 1970, the groovy Western Hotel & Casino, located downtown at Fremont St. and 9th St., closed down for good in January 2012. Originally a hotel and bingo parlor, upon its opening, the 8,925 sq. ft. property was the world's largest bingo hall, with 1,020 seats.

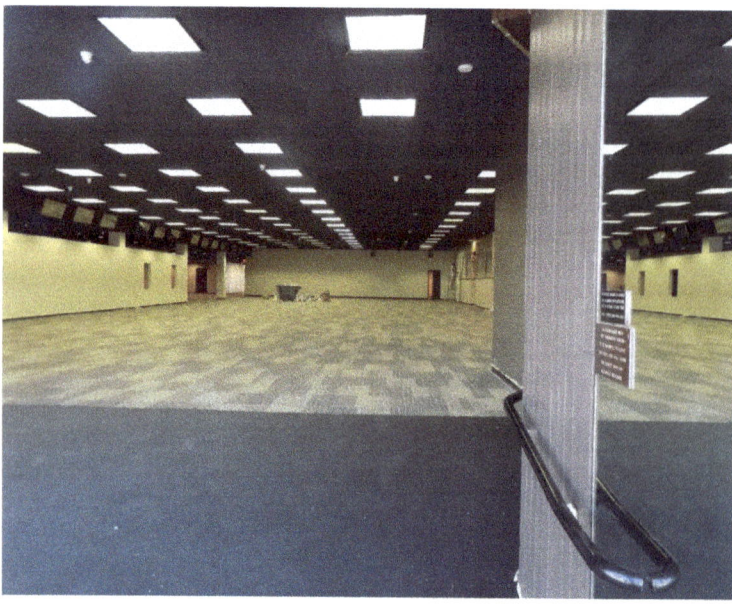

After changing ownership a few times over the years, in March 2013, the Western was purchased from the Tamares Group for $14 million as part of the Downtown Project, a campaign to gentrify the Fremont St. area. As of May 2015, the property remains vacant. Considering the fate of the numerous aforementioned motels and other properties purchased by the financially troubled Downtown Project, it's likely the Western will continue to sit abandoned for quite some time.

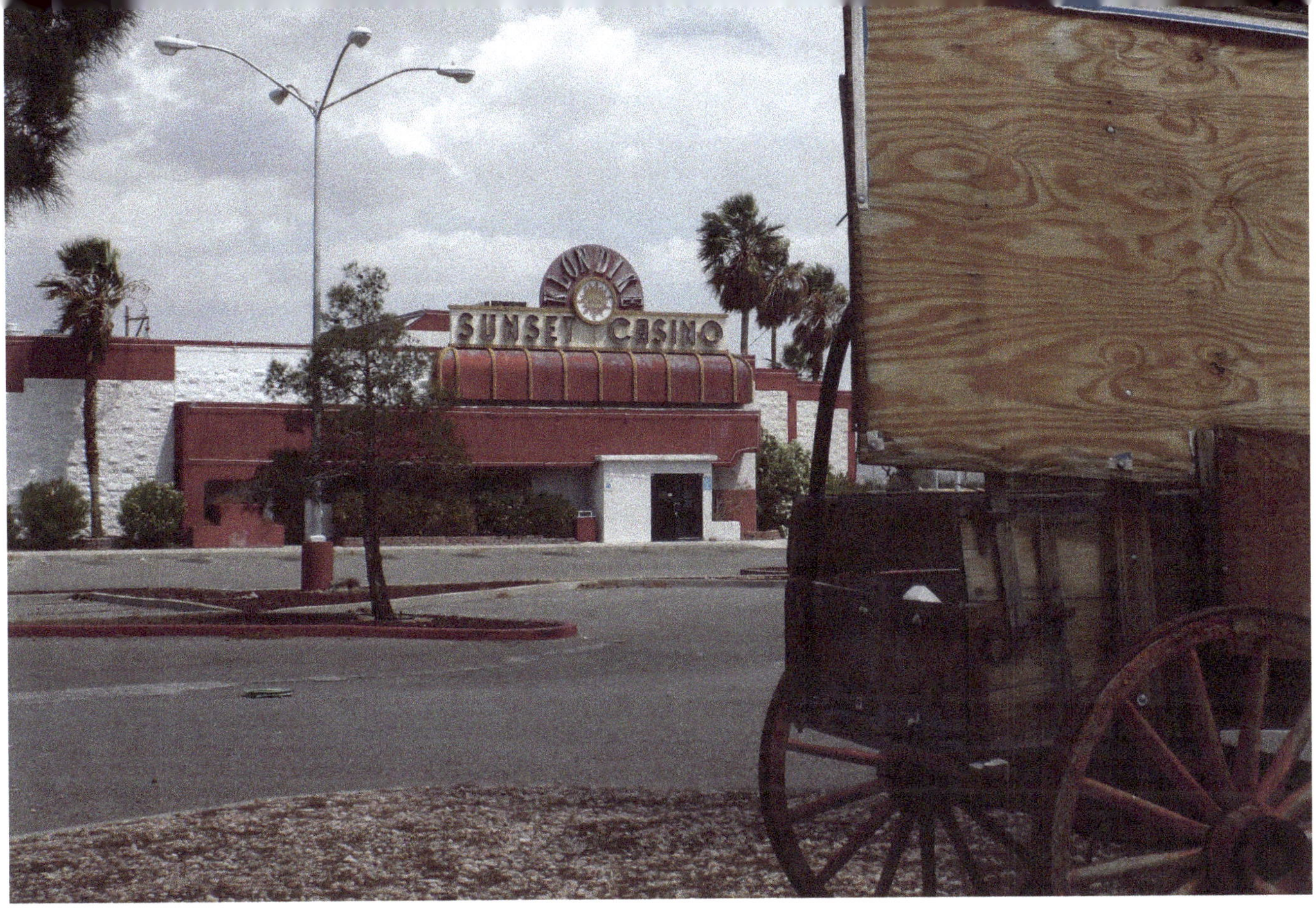

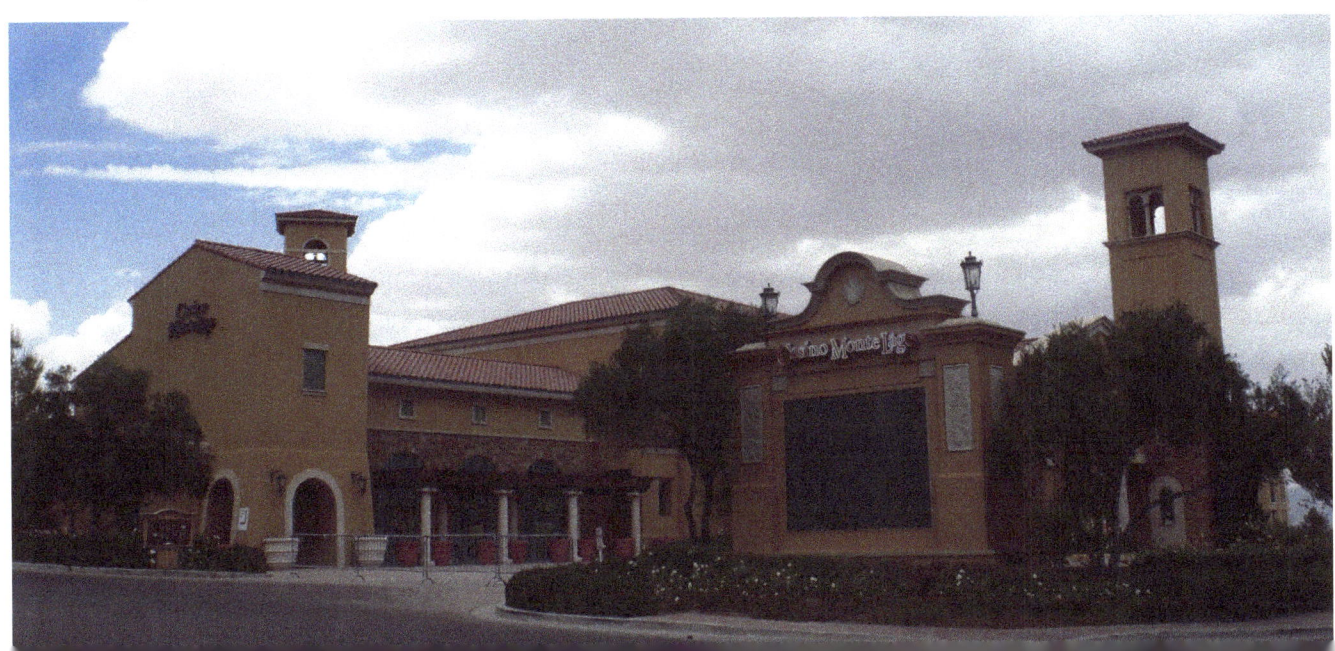

**Above:** Located at 444 W. Sunset Rd. in Henderson, the Klondike Sunset Casino was built in 1989 and closed in August 2014, a few months after its owner passed away. Purchased by CG Enterprises, there are plans to renovate/re-open the casino. Almost a year later, it's still vacant.

**Below:** Built in 2003, the Casino MonteLago at Lake Las Vegas shuttered in 2010 due to Recession woes. Purchased in November 2012 by the Kam Sang Co., the property has since been plagued by gaming permit issues. Owners plan to find an operator as soon as possible, yet as of May 2015, the property remains desolate.

# *stripped*

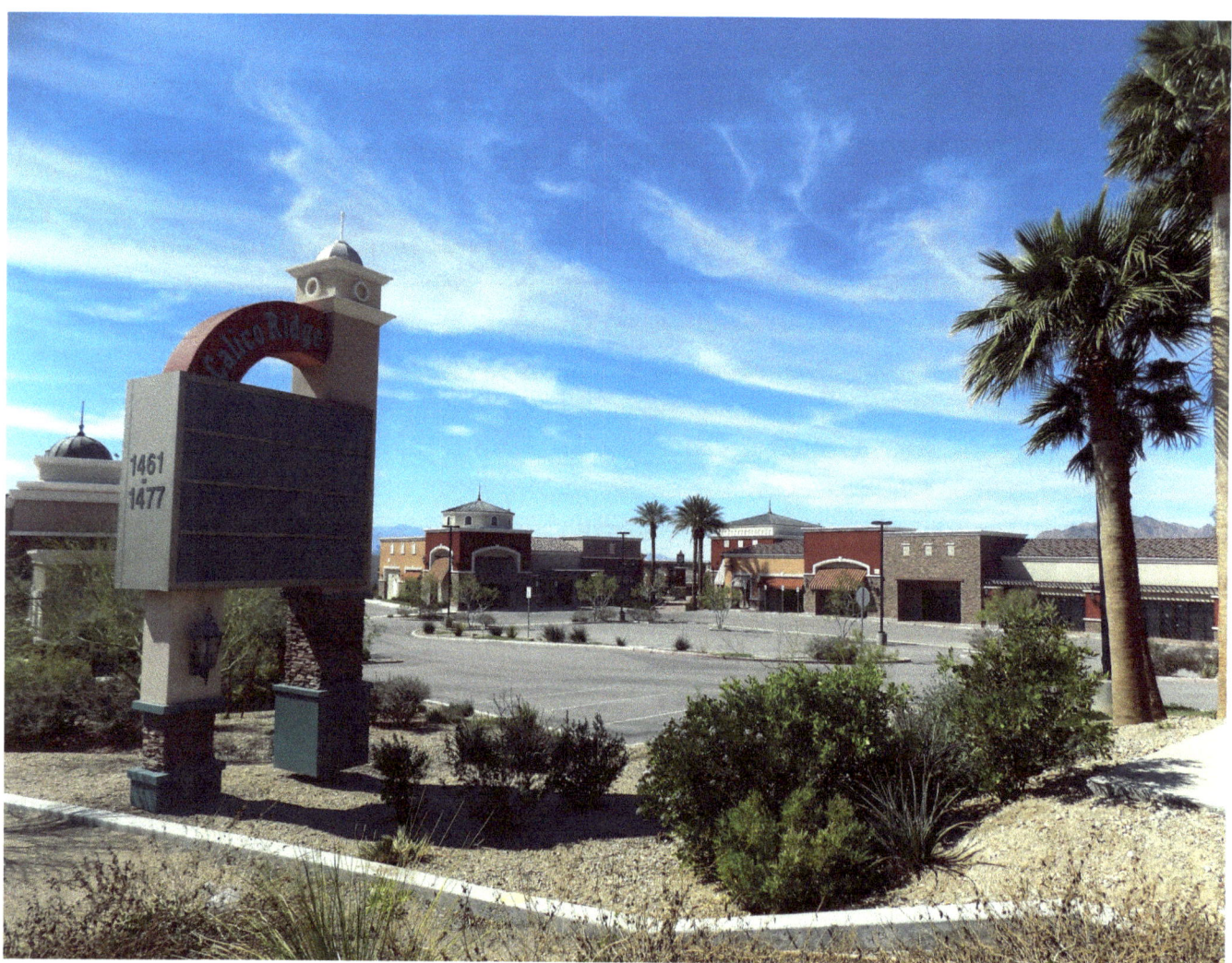

While driving around town, it is certain that every few blocks or so, you'll come across something abandoned. But then there are the times where you're just driving along, you turn a corner, and there it is: an entire strip mall...abandoned. It is surreal. While not as common as the one-off vacancies, there are quite a few completely (or almost completely) abandoned strip malls. Here are a few...

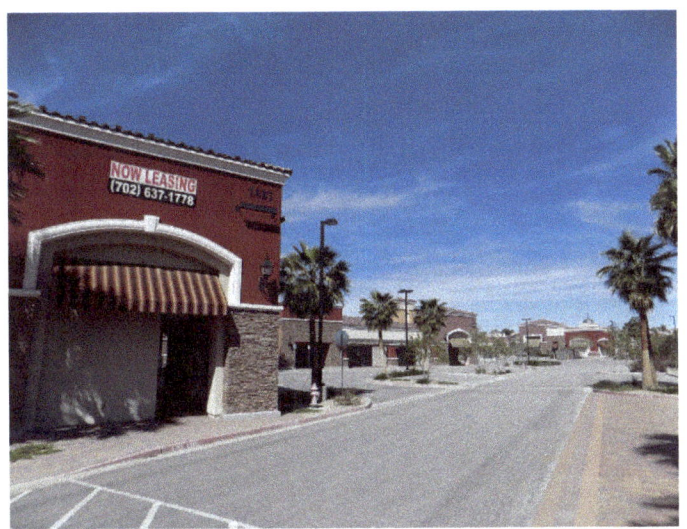

**Monument at Calico Ridge:** Located just west of Lake Las Vegas in Henderson and about a 25-30 minute drive east of the Strip, this completely uninhabited shopping plaza has the true feel of a ghost town. While many strip malls in Las Vegas have gone almost entirely vacant, there often remains at least one open store. Not the case here, as this facility never even opened its doors.

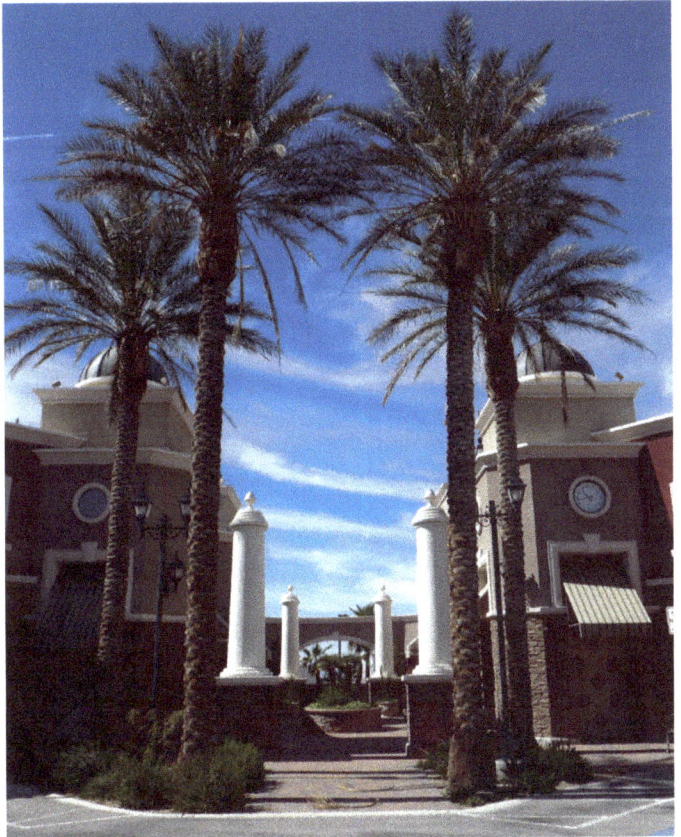

A cluster of 5 buildings, the upscale shopping center that never was sits somewhat isolated on Lake Mead Parkway, against a beautiful mountainous desert backdrop. Shoppers would've also been treated to a fantastic view of the Las Vegas Strip. With the exception of the steady howl of the desert winds, it is eerily silent. The ruffling feathers of a raven in a nearby palm tree and the hum of an occasional car whizzing by on the parkway a few yards from the fenced-off facility are the only sounds that break the desert silence.

The retail center is approximately 40,000 square feet and features 23 available retail spots. Construction on the project began in January 2008, and while it is completed, it continues to sit vacant. Currently owned by Calico Ridge Center LLC, the property was valued at $3.2 million in 2014.

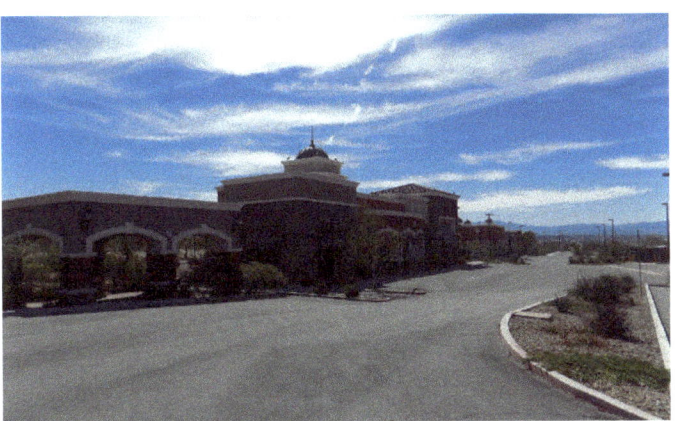

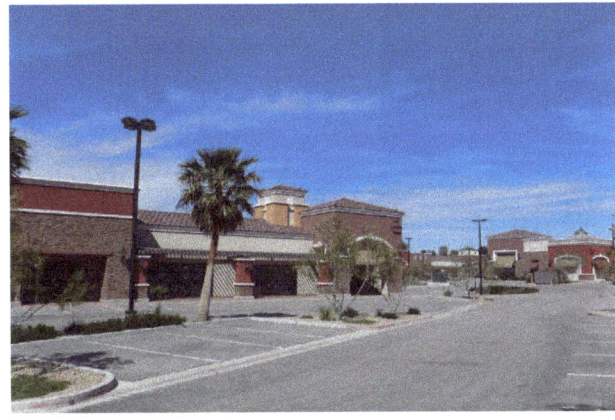

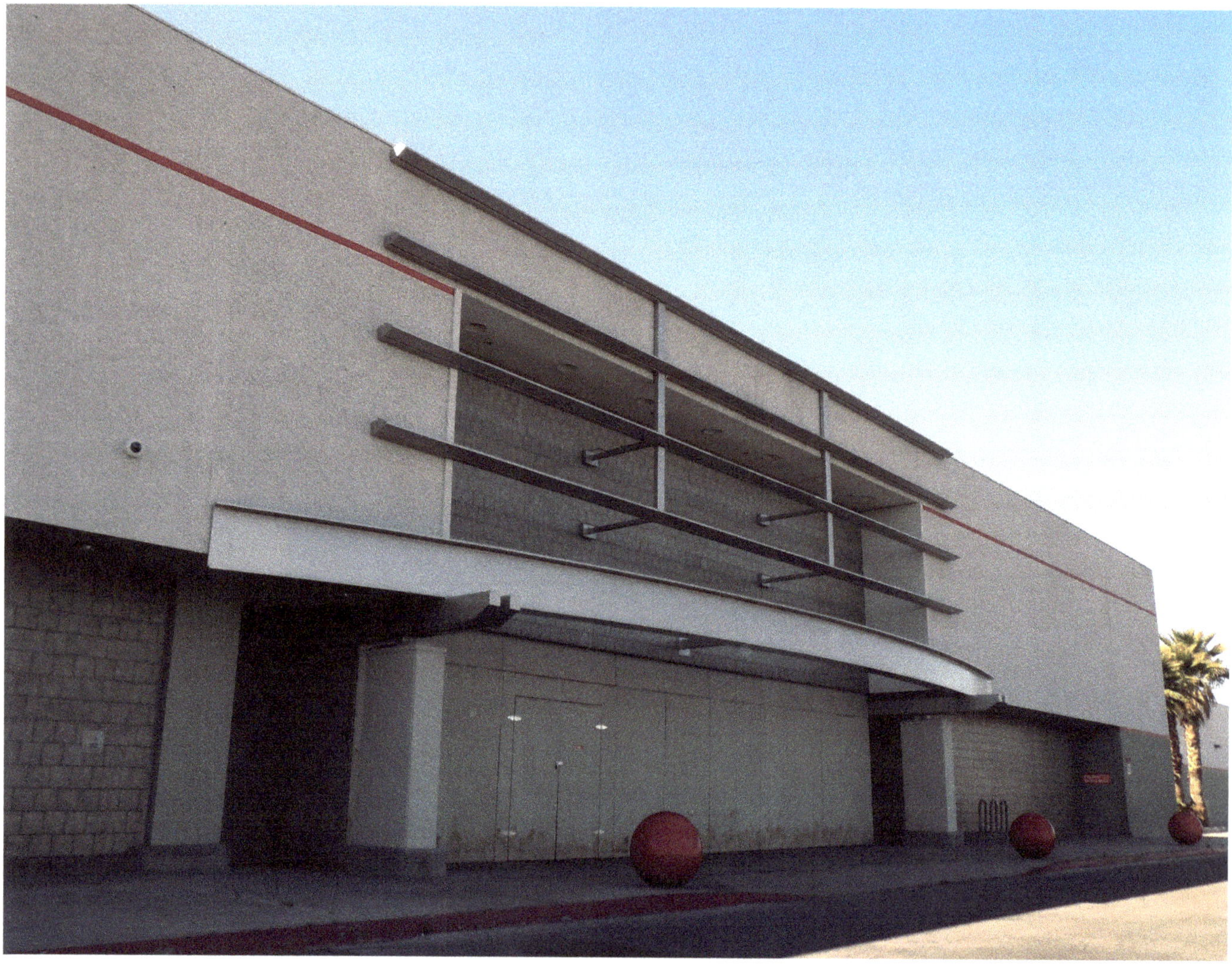

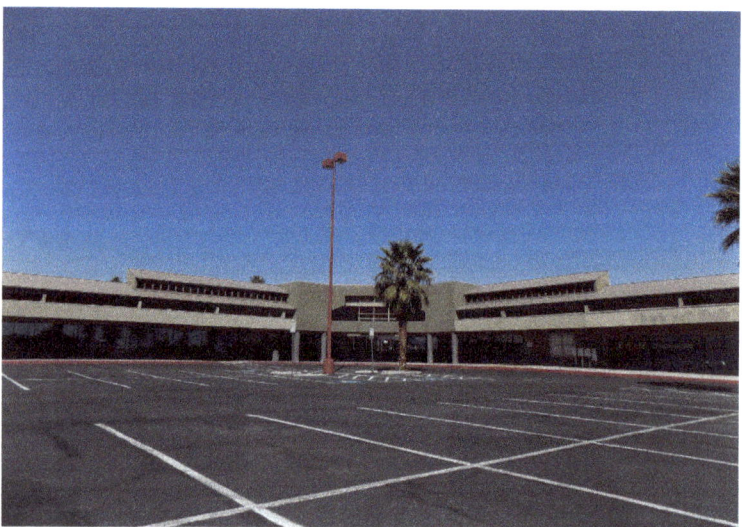

Even Target wasn't immune to the Recession in Las Vegas, as it closed this location at S. Decatur Blvd. and Meadows Ln. in May 2014. Along with Big Lots, Target once anchored the Decatur Crossing Center, and since the chains' departure, smaller retailers have also paid the price, as this strip mall now stands almost entirely vacant. But there's hope, as the Southern Nevada Health District has purchased the former Target and four adjacent storefronts for $6.5 mil for its headquarters and plans to move into the new facility by the end of 2015.

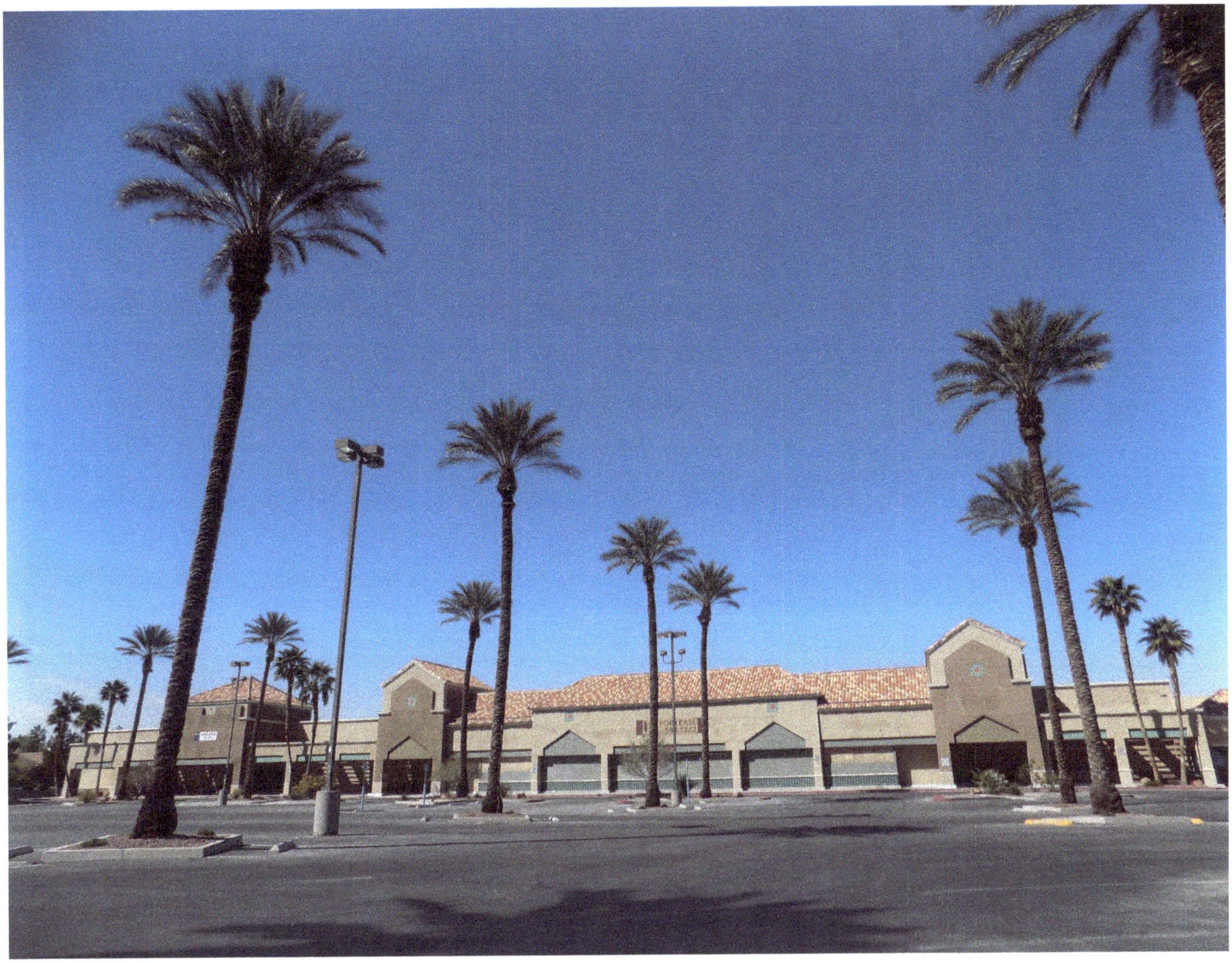

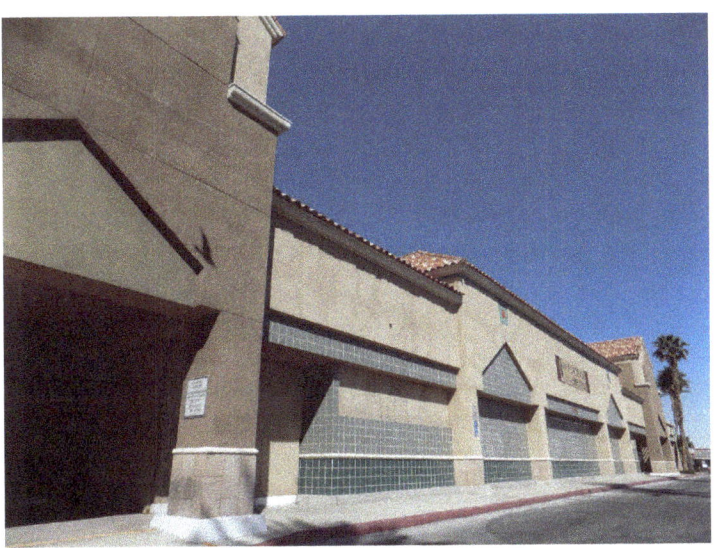

An Albertsons grocery store once anchored the Lake Mead Marketplace at Lake Mead Blvd. and Jones Blvd., but it closed shortly after the Recession hit. Some of the smaller stores hung on for awhile, but now the entire strip mall stands vacant. Former occupants included Blockbuster, Pizza Hut, the UPS Store, Jackson Hewitt Tax Services, Absolute Dental and China Joes.

# *partially stripped*

While not all strip malls have gone completely desolate, virtually every strip mall in town has been hit, and within each lay at least one or two vacancies:

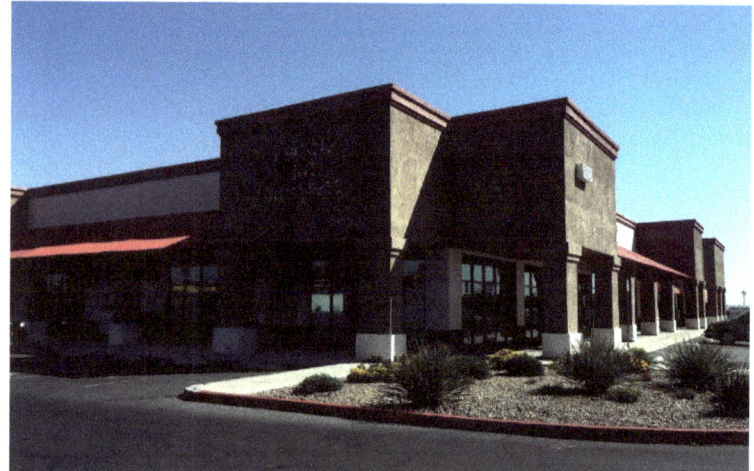

This strip mall at Sahara Ave. and Rainbow Blvd. is just another hit by hard times. Its former occupants included medical supply store U.S. Med, baby furniture and supply store Dagerman's Just for Kids, a RacerX sports apparel store, a shoe store, music store, furniture store and full-service salon.

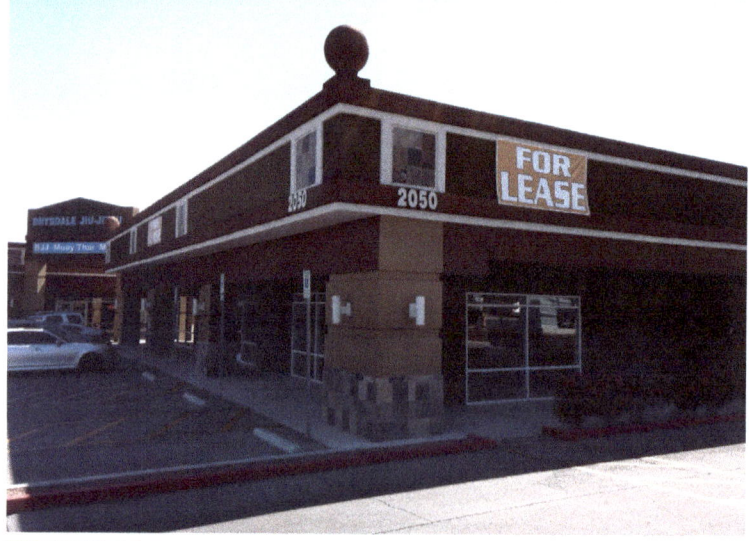

This location on Rainbow Blvd., just north of Sahara Ave., was formerly home to Las Vegas Office Furniture and custom doormaker Bella Grande Entrances.

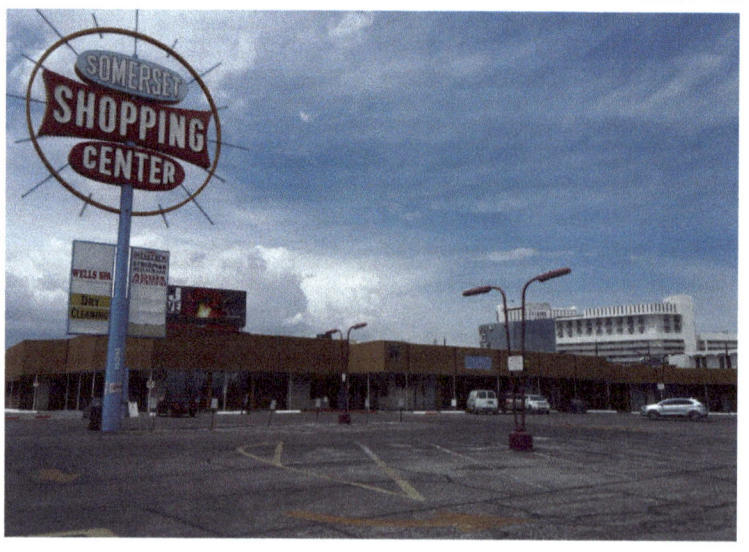

Built in 1966, Somerset Shopping Center is almost completely abandoned. Located on Convention Center Dr. (across from the site of the now-razed Clarion Hotel), the 3.2 acre parcel is a quick walk to the Strip, Convention Center and monorail. The property hasn't been purchased, awaiting demo; they just can't get tenants. With the glut of available Strip-adjacent retail space, potential renters are likely considering newer properties.

One of the more famous casualties of the Recession, Circuit City went bankrupt in 2009, closing all its locations. While many of its locations have already been re-occupied, this relic of the Recession, located by Sahara Ave. and Decatur Blvd., sits almost untouched six years later.

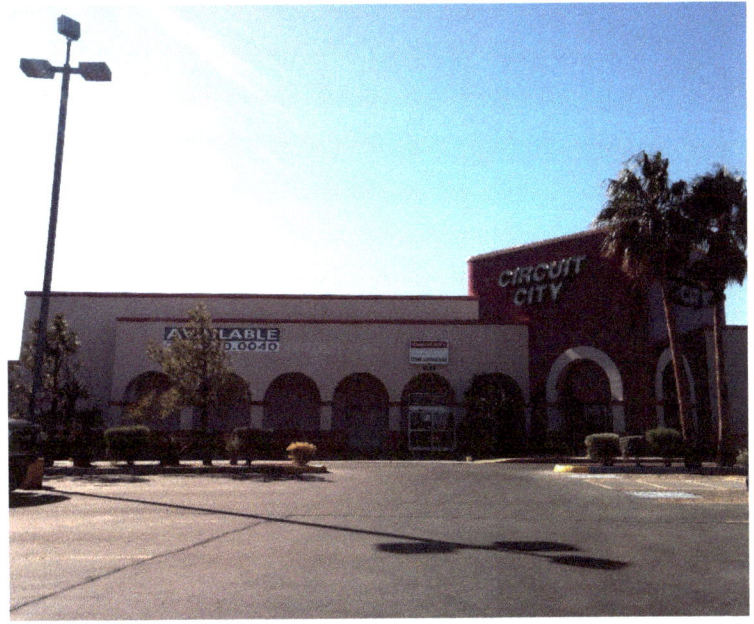

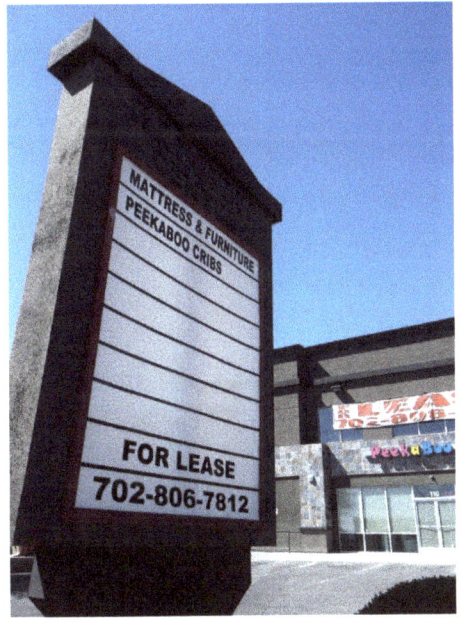

The Rainbow Center, on Rainbow Blvd. just north of Sahara Ave., once housed a divorce lawyer, bridal store and physical therapy office. While those are all gone, there are some new tenants - but as evidenced from the sign, there's still quite a bit of space available for lease.

Albertsons had closed a handful of its stores throughout Las Vegas during the Recession years, but as of 2015, over 30 locations still remain. This location at S. Maryland Parkway and E. Sahara Avenue was closed in February 2014.

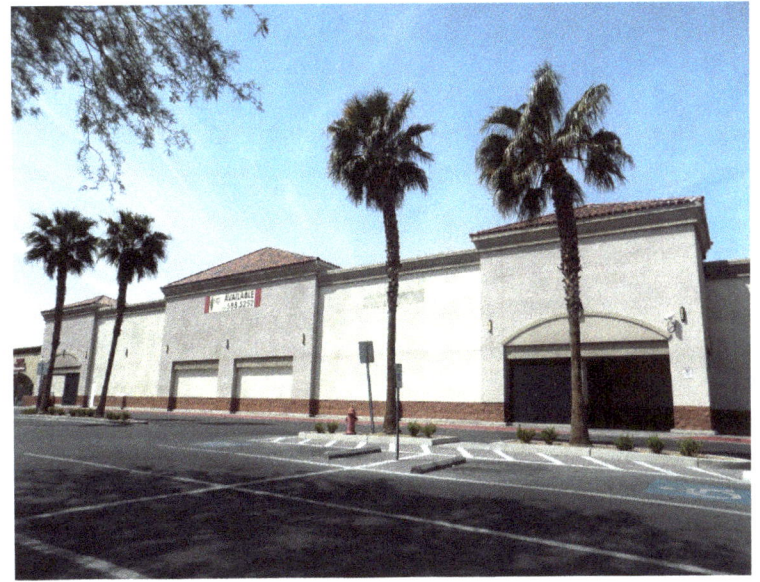

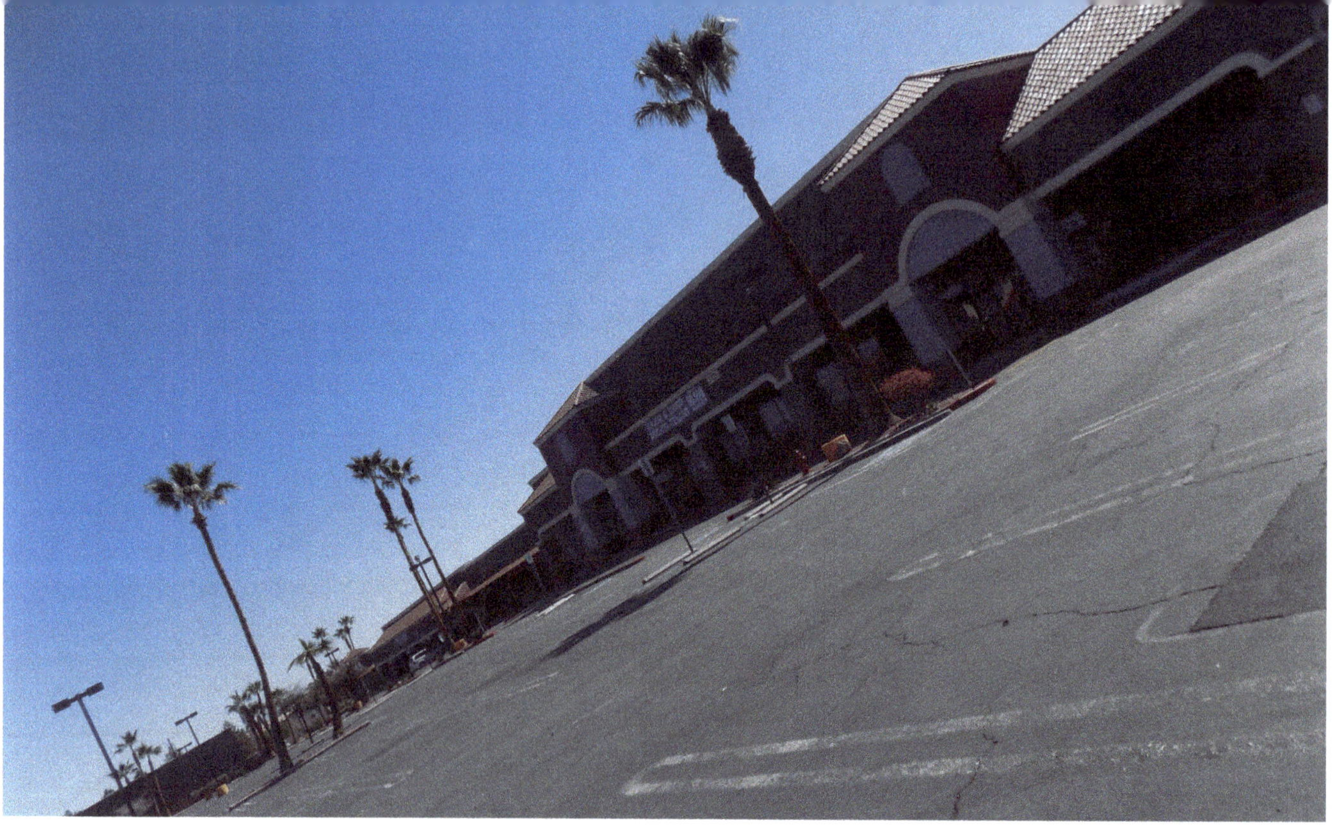

**Above:** Retail arts and crafts store Michael's and grocery store Vons once anchored the Pecos Plaza at S. Pecos Rd. and E. Russell Rd. The strip mall is now almost entirely vacant.

**Below:** Built in 1967, this property on E. Sahara Ave., just west of Eastern Ave., had been occupied by the Ford Motor Co. from 1979 to 2012. Gaudin Ford relocated to a smaller facility near the 215 West Freeway and Rainbow Blvd. After three years vacant, the facility is set to be the future home of the Champions Baseball Academy in 2015.

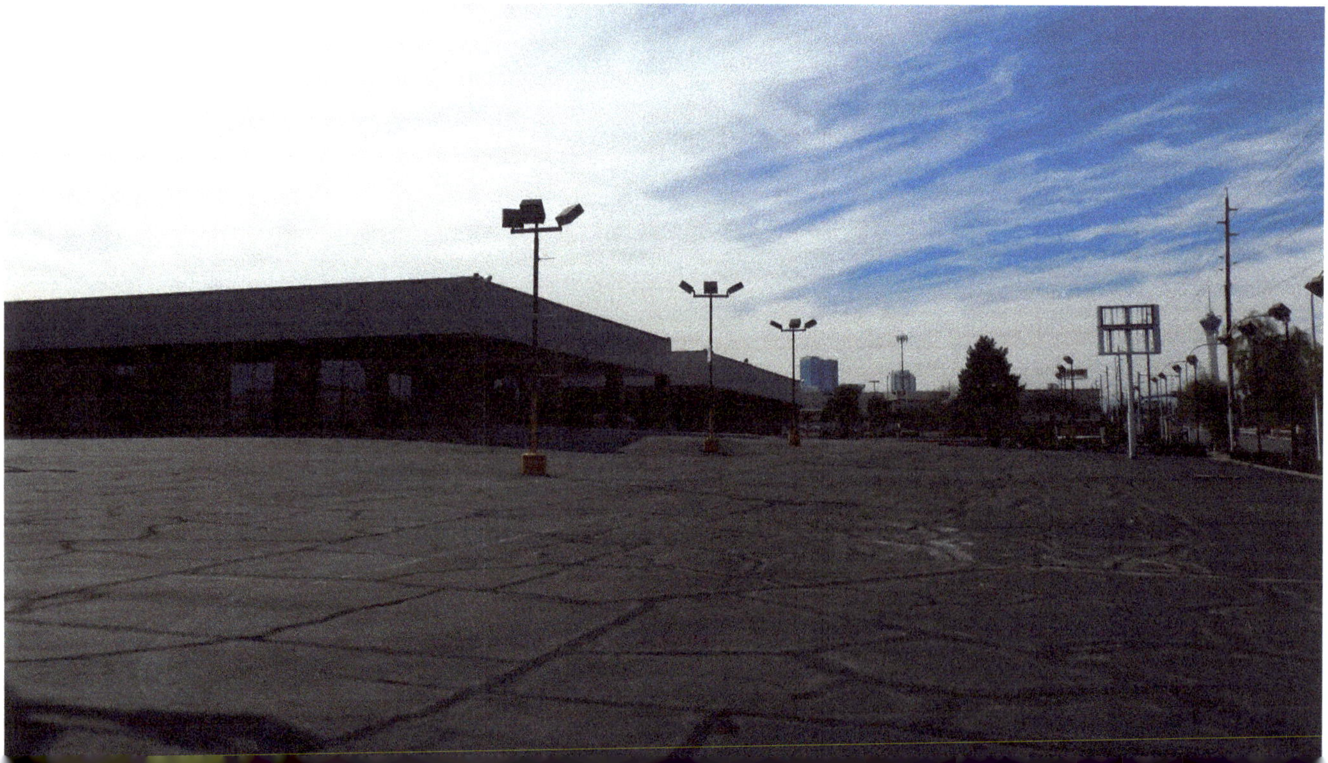

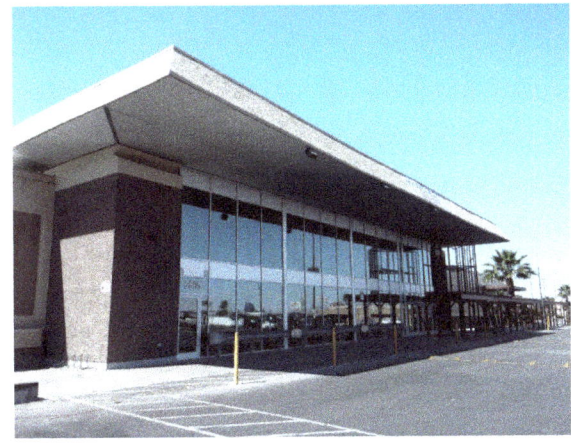

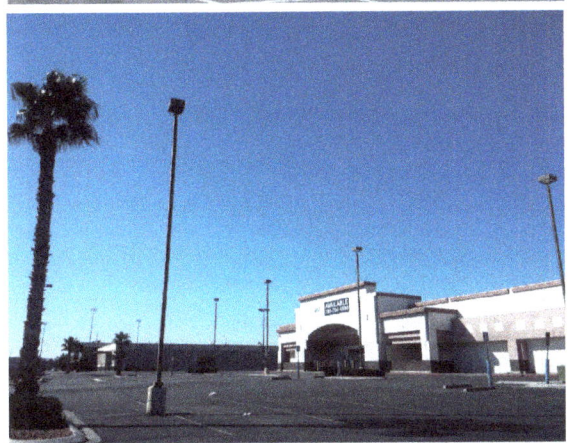

A few short minutes east of the Strip, at E. Sahara Ave. and Eastern Ave., this shopping center lost its two anchors, with the Harley-Davidson store (left) closing in late 2014, followed by its neighbor Food4Less, which shuttered in January 2015.

Harley-Davidson relocated to a smaller facility on the Strip. Food4Less closed all its Vegas locations. The Smith's grocery store chain is set to take over a few of the locations formerly occupied by Food4Less, but this isn't one of them.

Plans for either vacant facility (below, Harley on left, Food4Less, right) in this retail center remain unknown.

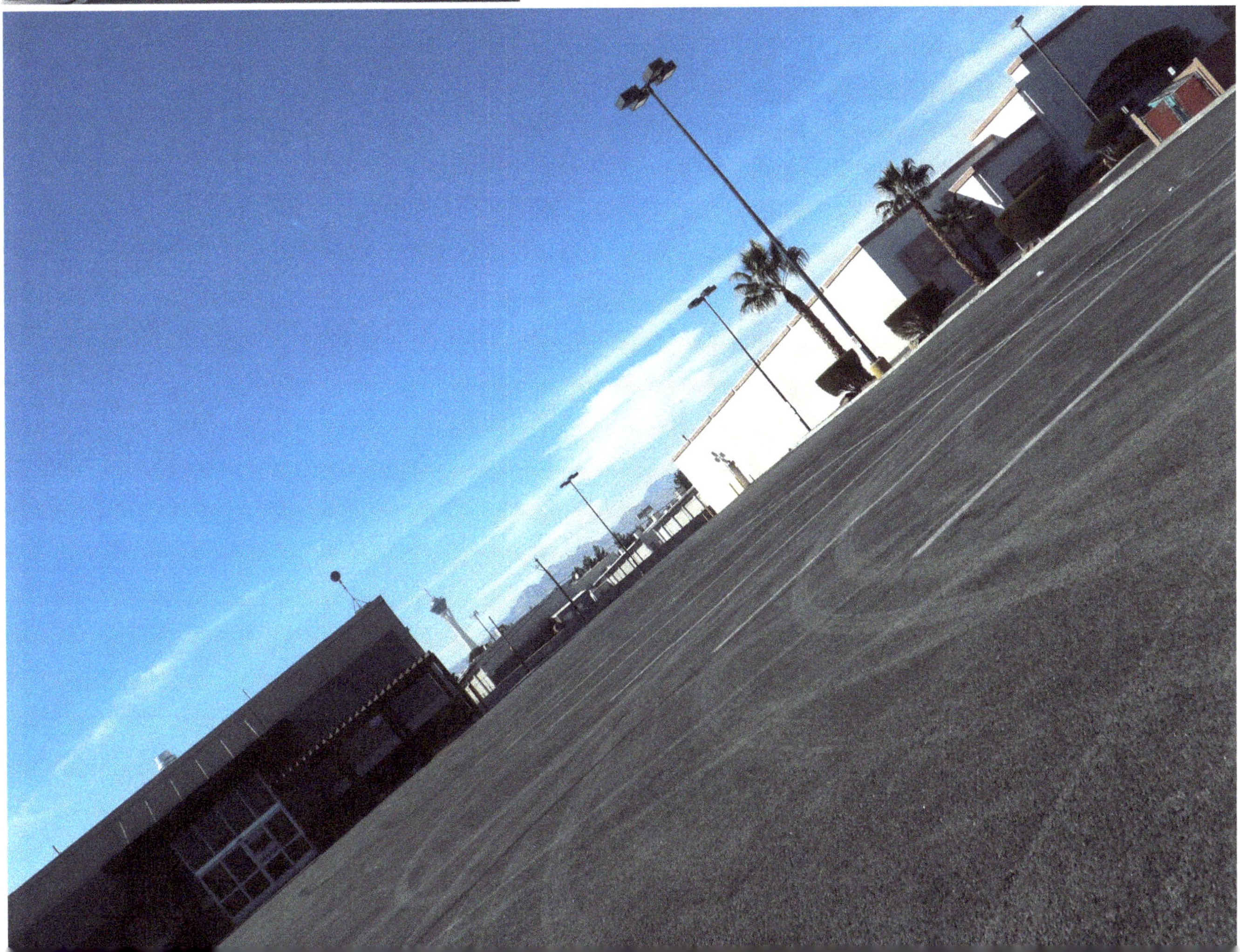

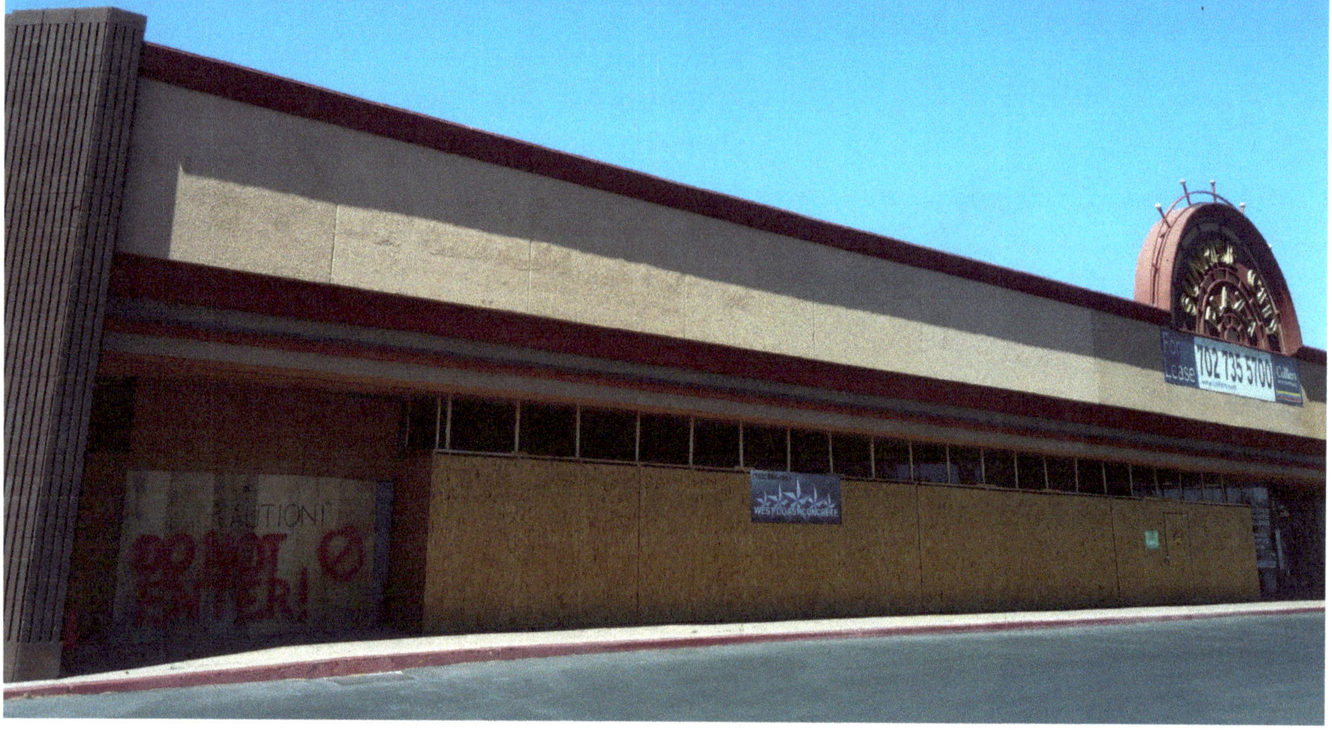

**Above:** Of the approximately 20 retail spots at the Sunrise City Plaza strip mall on S. Maryland Pkwy., south of Karen Ave., most of the local or independent retailers have vanished. Left behind are Sam Ash music store, Big 5 Sporting Goods, OfficeMax and Impress printers.

**Below:** Also located in the Sunrise City Plaza strip mall, the short-lived Hacienda Del Rey restaurant opened in 2013 and closed in March 2015. The location had been previously occupied by another Mexican restaurant, El Patron.

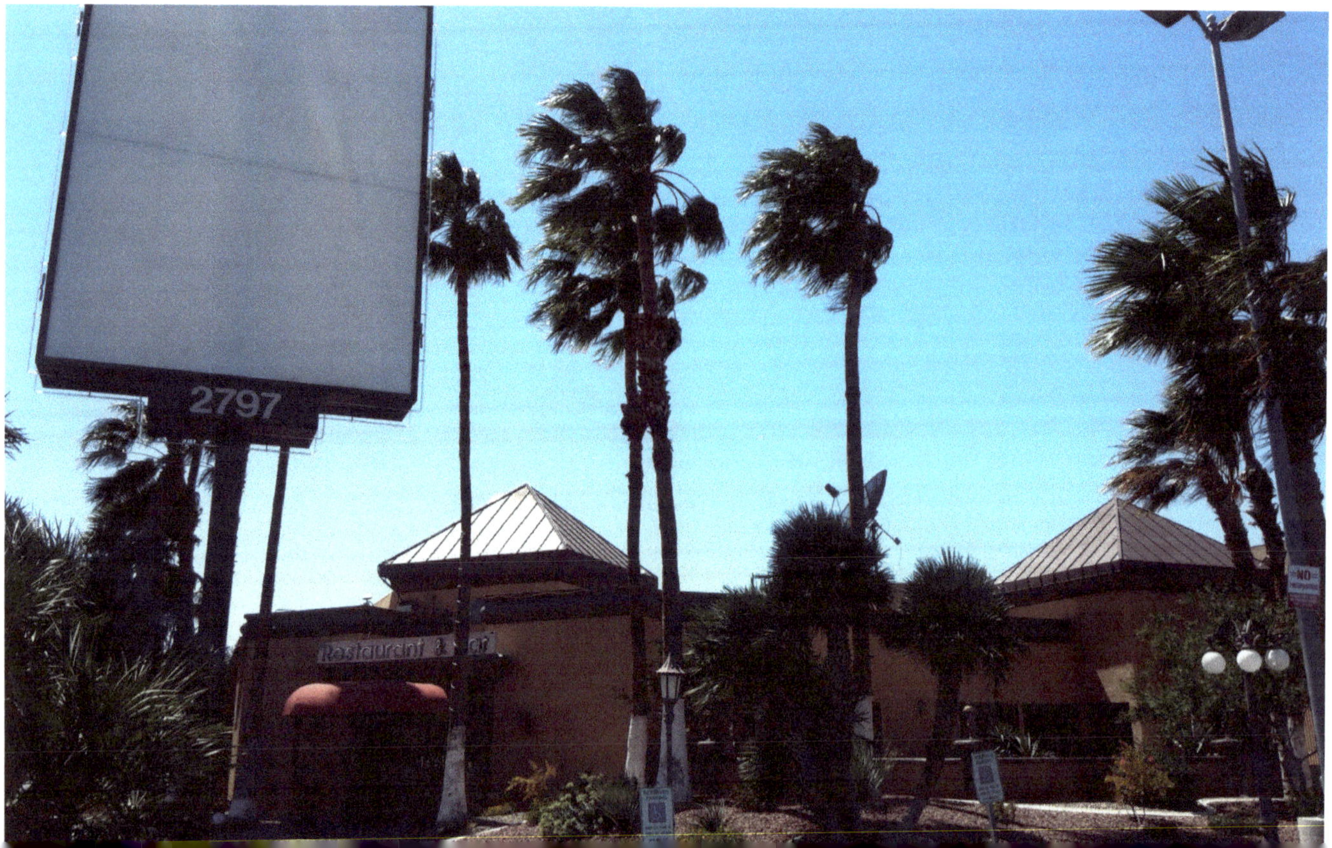

# *clubbed*

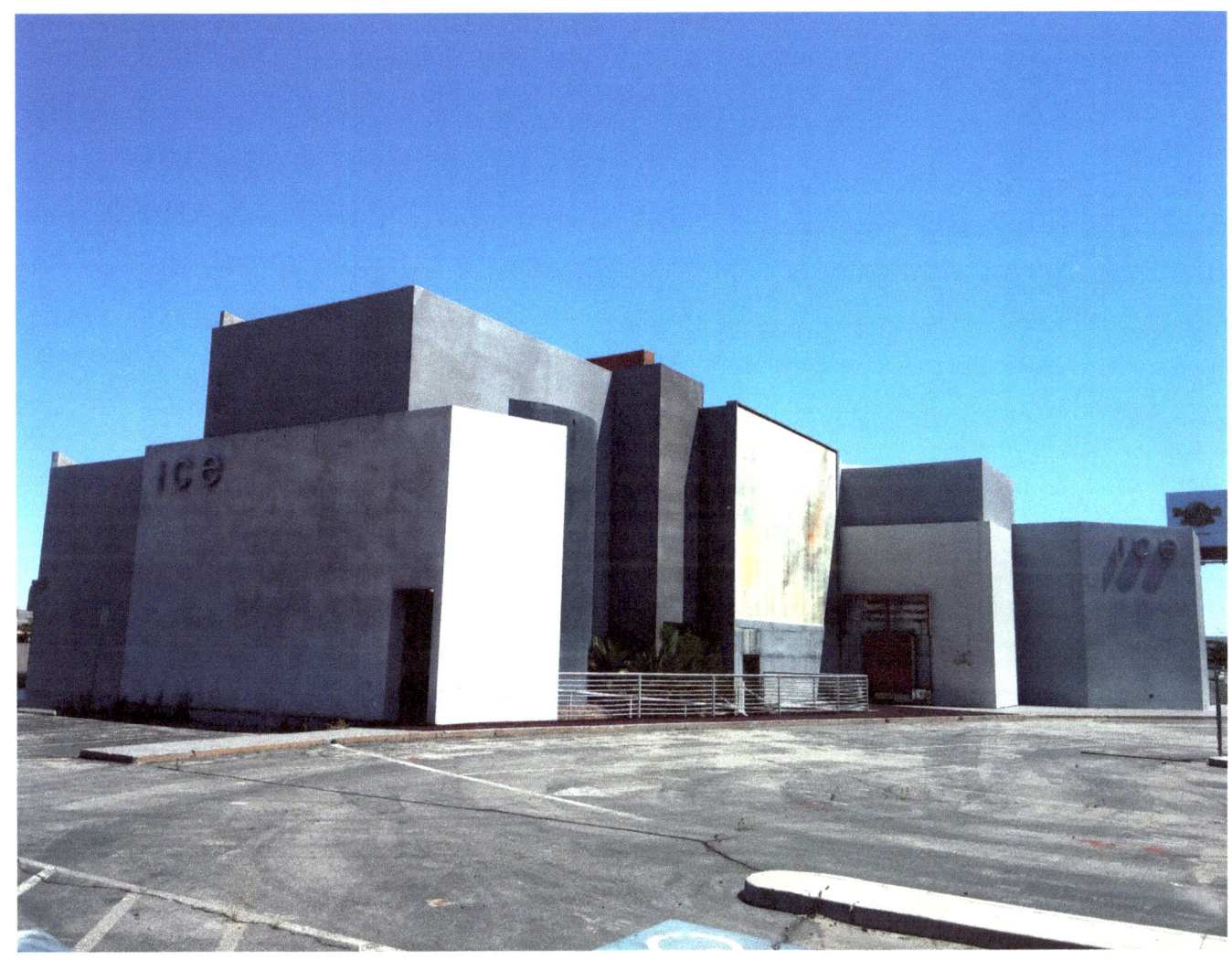

Many nightclubs in Vegas have come and gone, often quickly replaced by a similar but new reincarnation. Not the case with Ice.

Located at Harmon Ave. and Koval Ln., Ice nightclub has been sitting vacant for almost nine years. Its demise, a byproduct of the Recession, came in October 2006, when Edge Investment Group purchased the 21-acre parcel of land where Ice is located. Edge partnered with Starwood Resorts to build the $1.7 billion W Hotel. Recession blues set in, and that never happened.

Just one block east of the Strip (and roughly a block south of where famed rapper Tupac Shakur was gunned down and killed in Sept. 1996), the club still remains, fenced-off, with a sign out front that reads "This property is intended to be used for a Casino and Resort hotel." It's fair to assume land owners would be open to other alternatives, as there are currently no plans in development for the property.

# closed for business

A smattering of other retailers around town that have closed shop...the three pictured on this page are located on E. Sahara Ave., just a few blocks east of the Strip. (Top, left: The Presidential Shave Shop; Top, right: Nevada Coin Mart; Bottom: Sci-Fi Center)

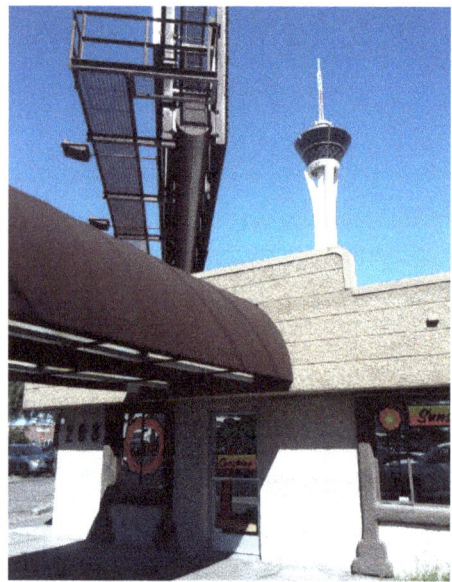

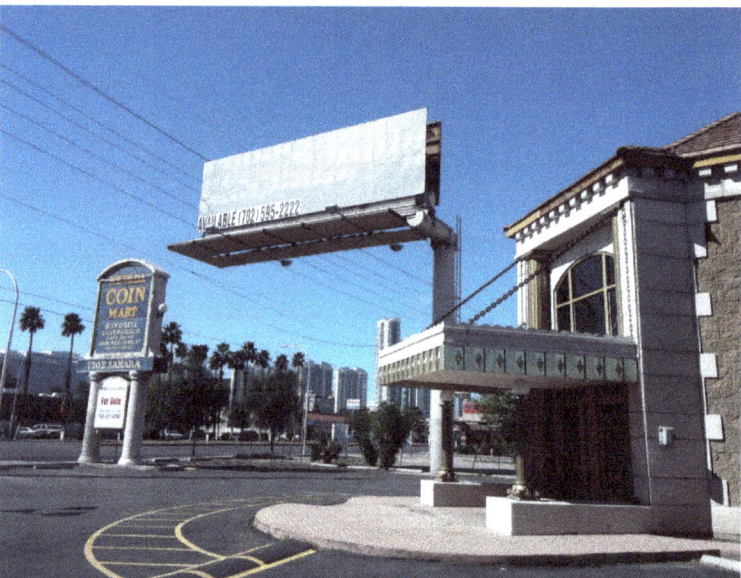

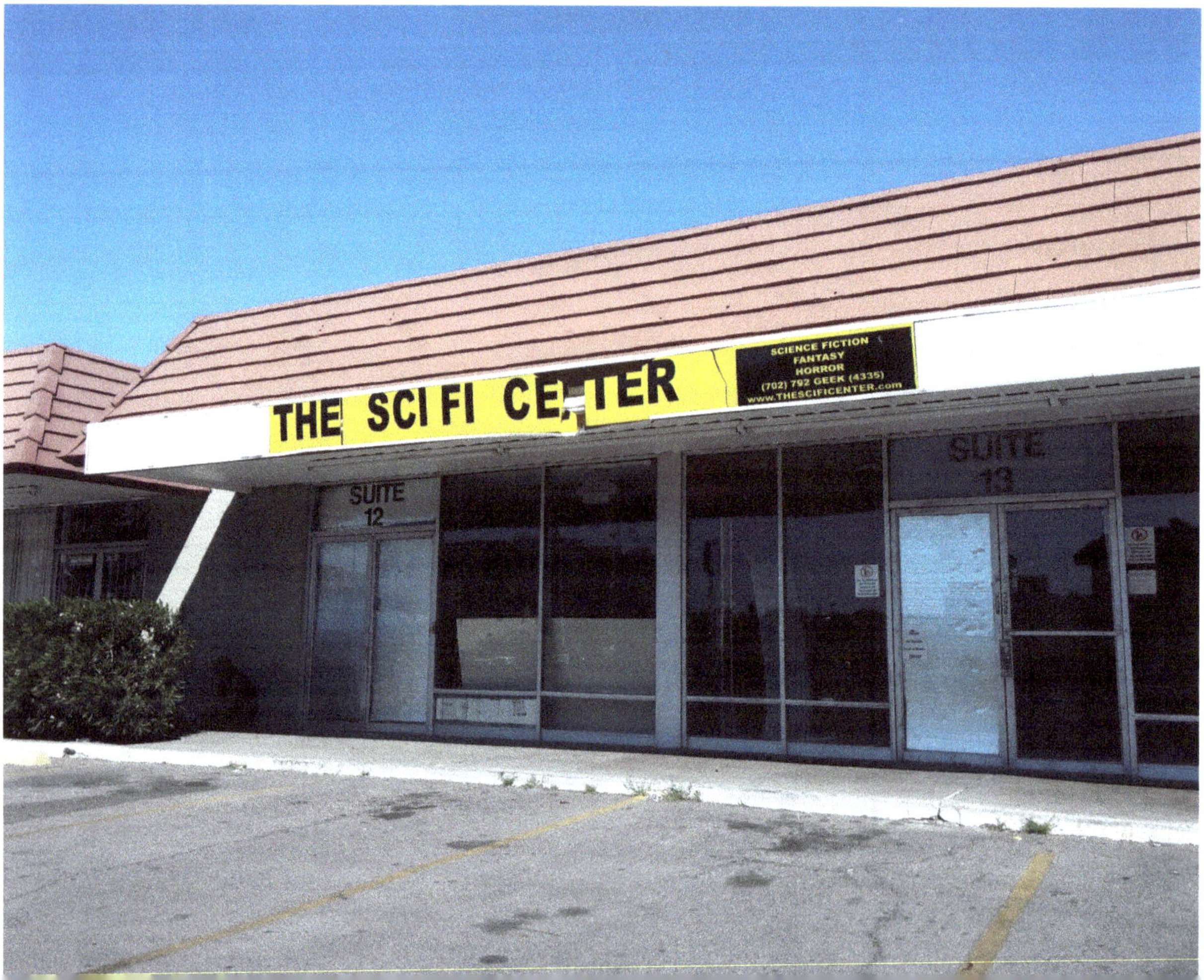

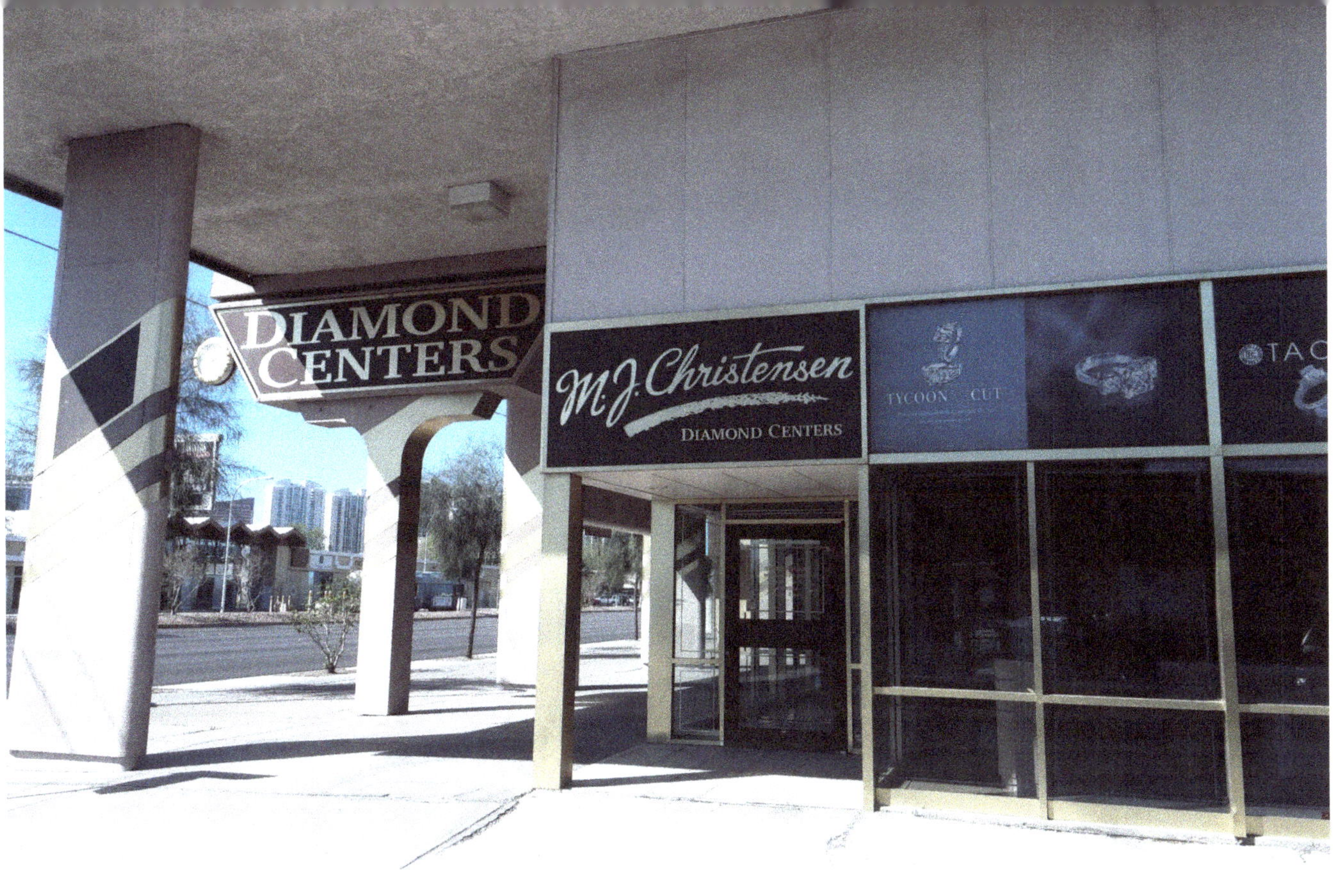

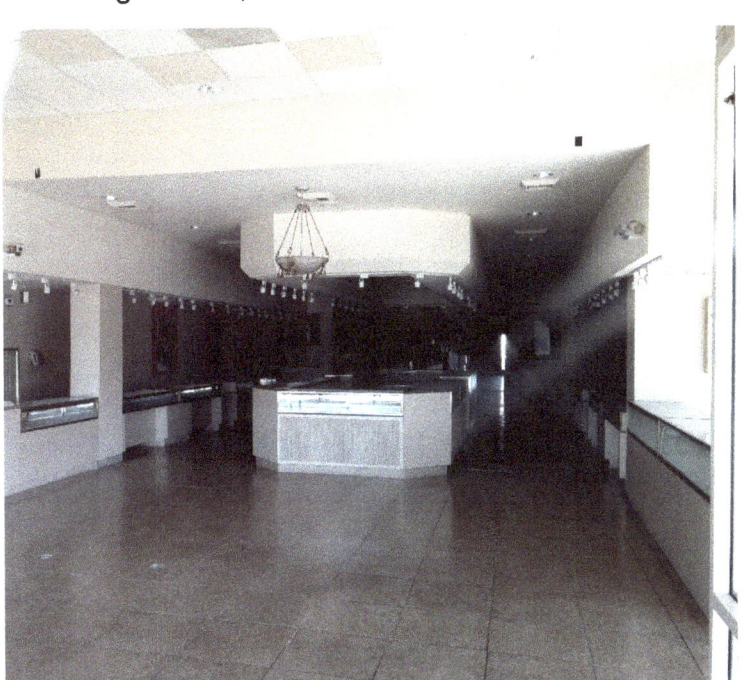

**Above:** Diamonds may be a girl's best friend, but apparently not during the Recession, as evidenced by this abandoned Diamond Centers, located on E. Sahara Ave., just west of S. Maryland Parkway.

**Below:** (Left) No more diamonds for sale at the desolate Diamond Centers. (Right) With the glut of newer development available throughout town, older facilities, like the defunct Strip Centre on Las Vegas Blvd., have suffered.

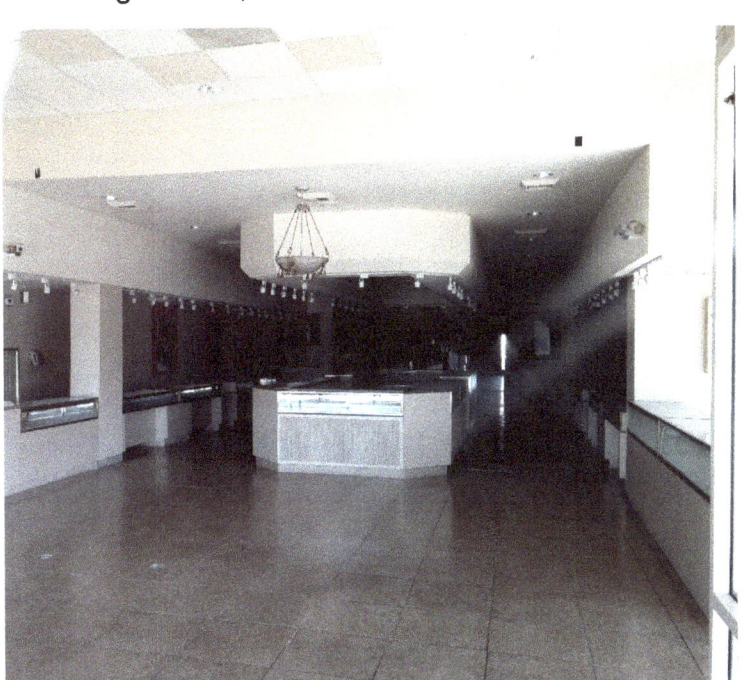
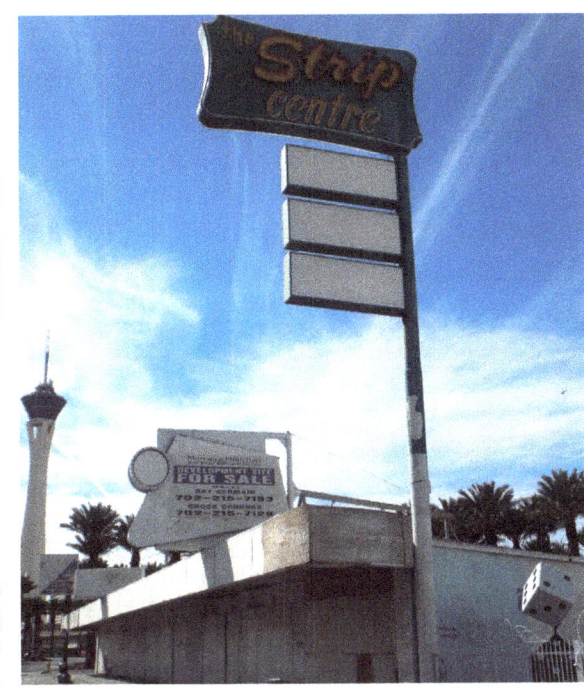

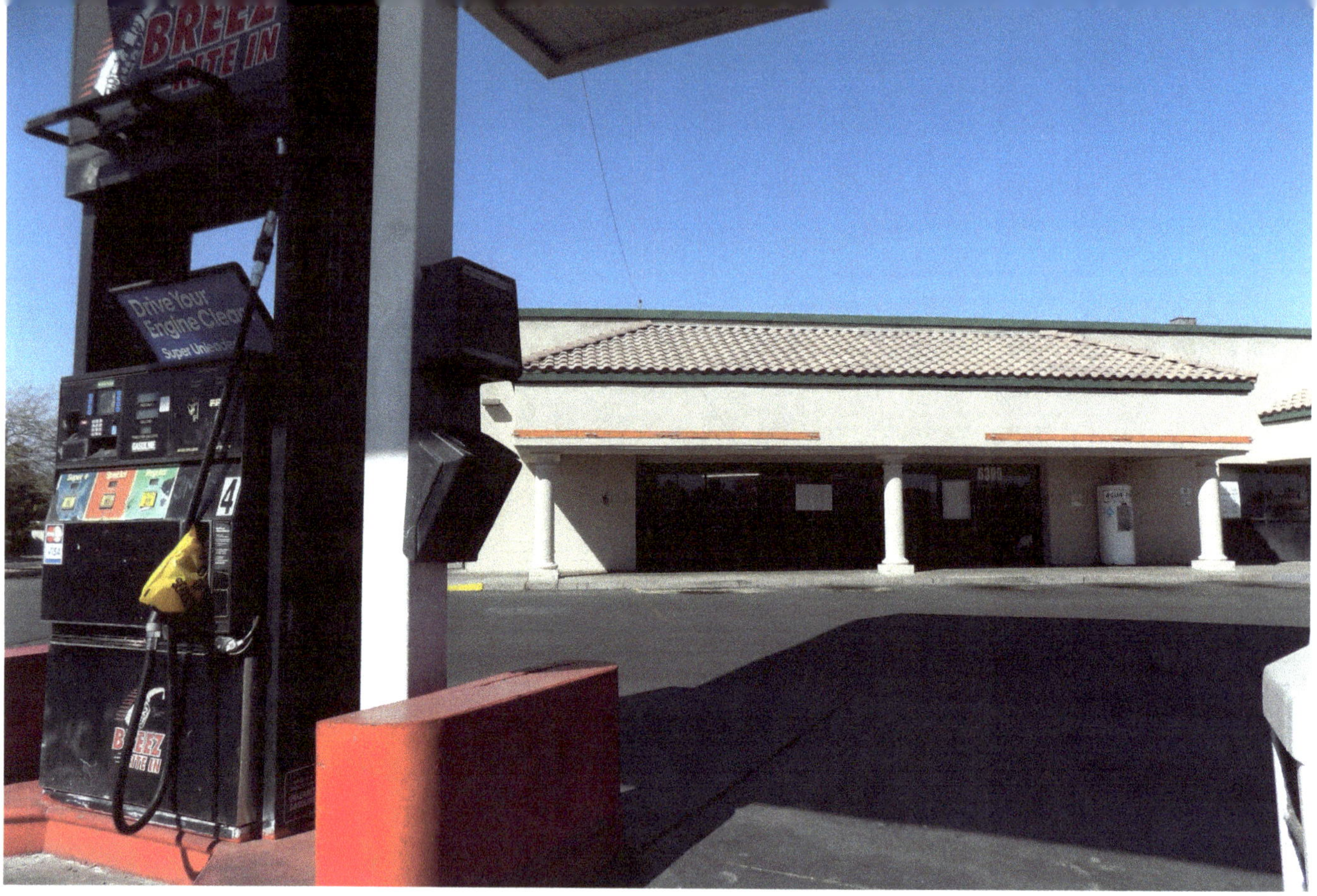

**Above:** Breez Rite In gas station/convenience store at W. Lake Mead Blvd. & Torrey Pines Dr.
**Below:** Part of the Station Plaza at Texas Station, on W. Lake Mead Blvd., east of N. Rancho Dr.

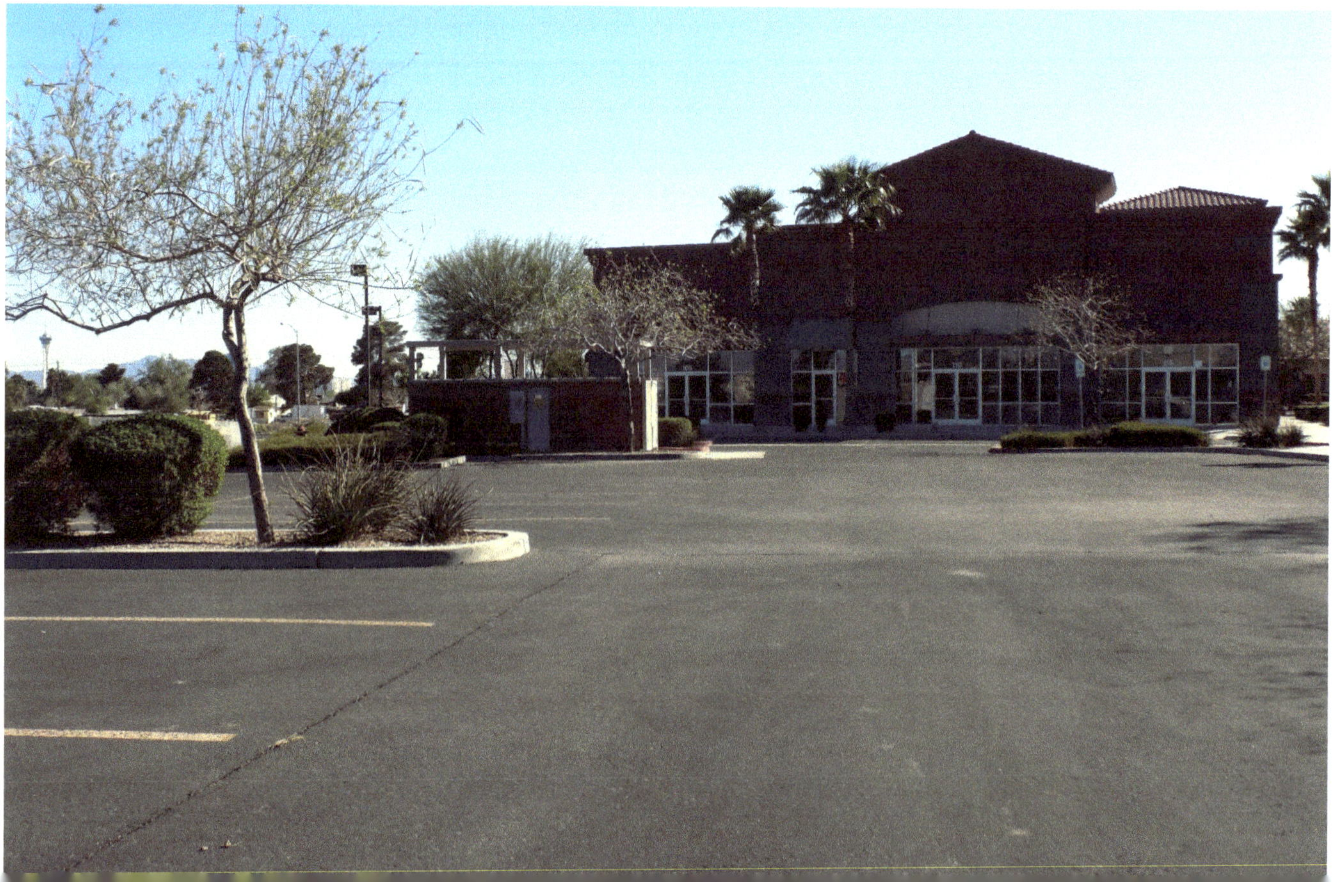

# _kitchen's closed_

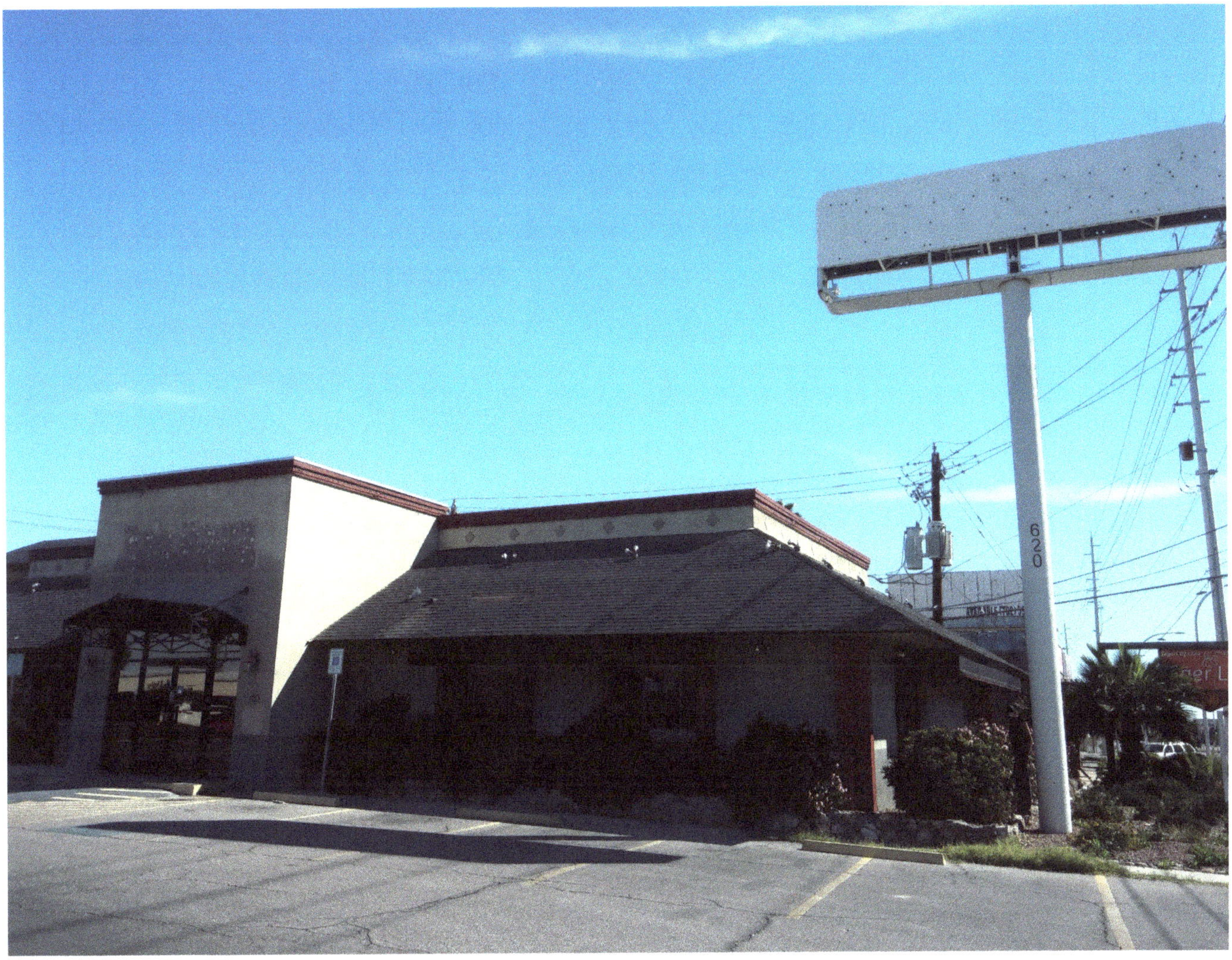

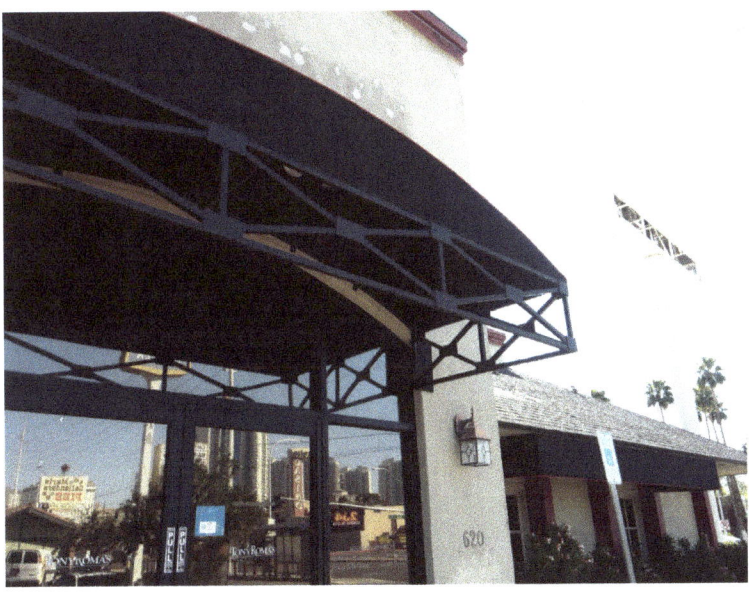

Fans of mob history will likely recognize this now-defunct Tony Roma's restaurant, which closed in 2013, on Sahara Ave., just east of the Strip. In 1982, Frank "Lefty" Rosenthal and his Cadillac fell victim to a car bombing, right here in this very parking lot. The reputed mobster, a former Stardust executive at the time of the attack, survived the blast by quickly jumping from the vehicle. No suspect was ever identified.

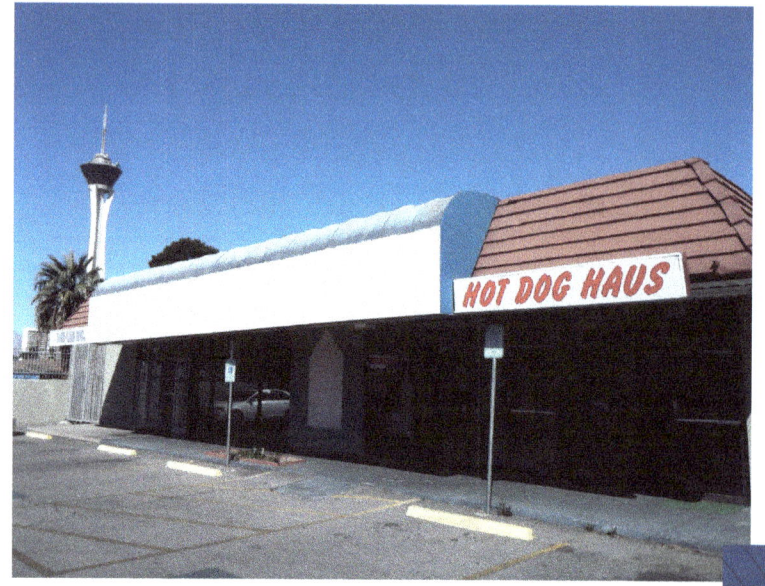

What!? Not the Hot Dog Haus. Closed in 2012, this location is situated in the same plaza as the aforementioned Tony Roma's and Sci Fi Center. To the left of the Hot Dog Haus, German restaurant Cafe Heidelberg ended its 40-year run in June 2012, unable to negotiate new lease terms with the property owner. As of mid-2015, both locations are still vacant.

No laughing matter, closed in late 2009, the Laughing Jackalope Motel Bar & Grill sits desolate on the dying east side of the South Strip, just across from the prosperous Mandalay Bay Hotel & Casino. All that remains of the Jackalope is a concrete pad where the motel once stood, a vacant building with graffiti and boarded-up windows, a few homeless people and a tattered sign.

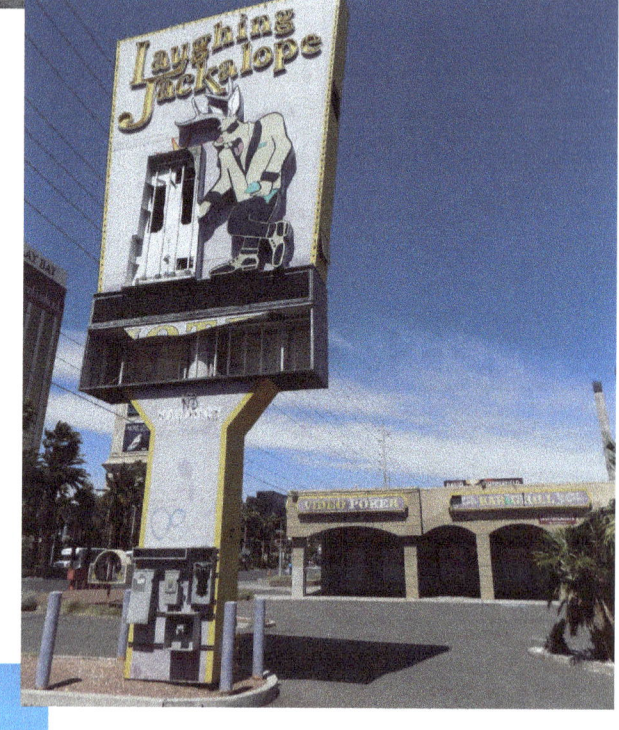

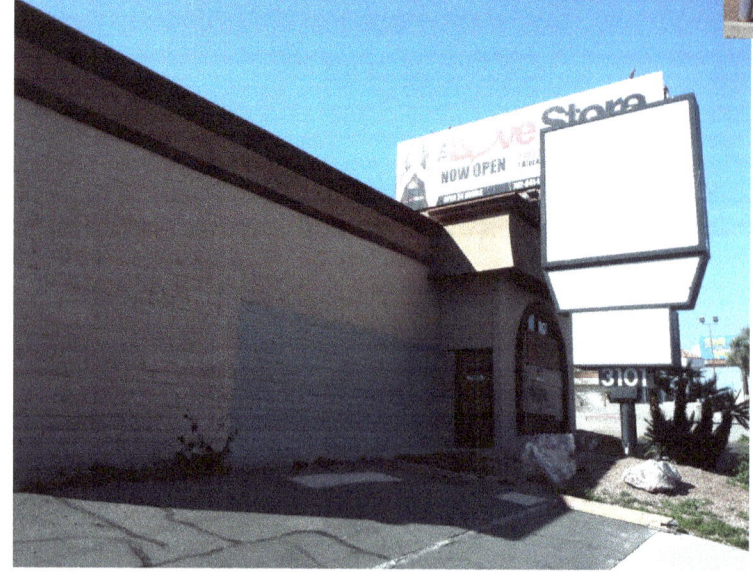

The Red Room Bar & Grill, located on W. Sahara Blvd. a few blocks west of the I-15, closed during the summer of 2009.

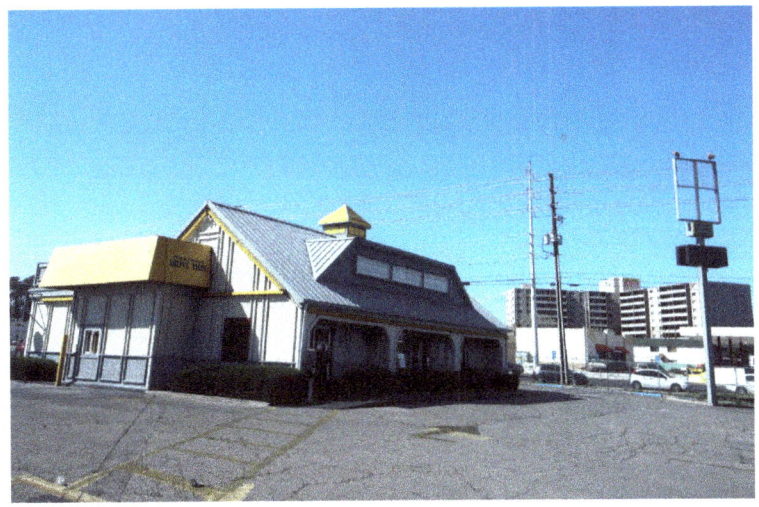

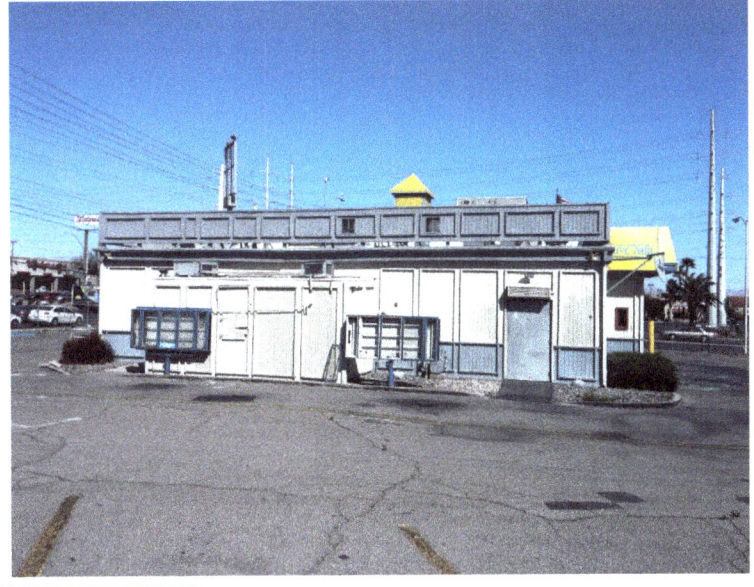

Be careful not to blink, things can change in a flash. The top two shots here of this vacant Long John Silver's at S. Maryland Parkway and E. Flamingo Rd. were taken in March 2015. Within weeks, the fast food restaurant had been razed (below), and all that remained was this empty lot and the chain's tattered sign. (Guess fast fried fish really wasn't a hit in the desert.)

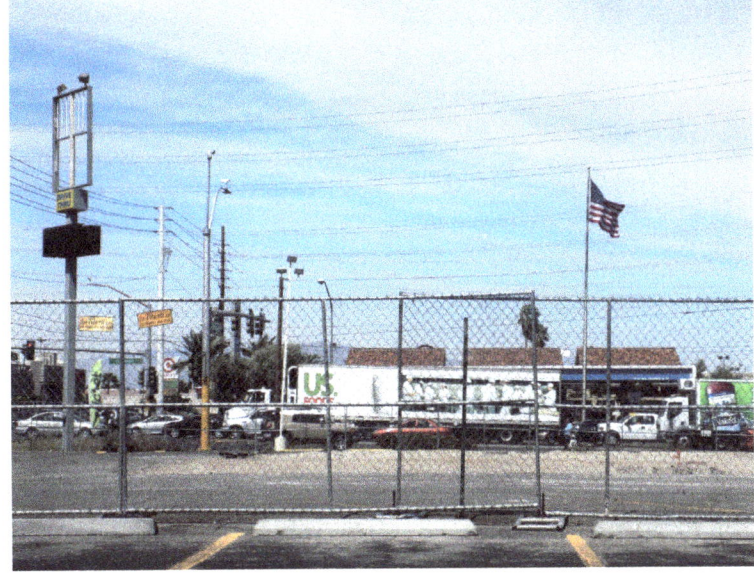

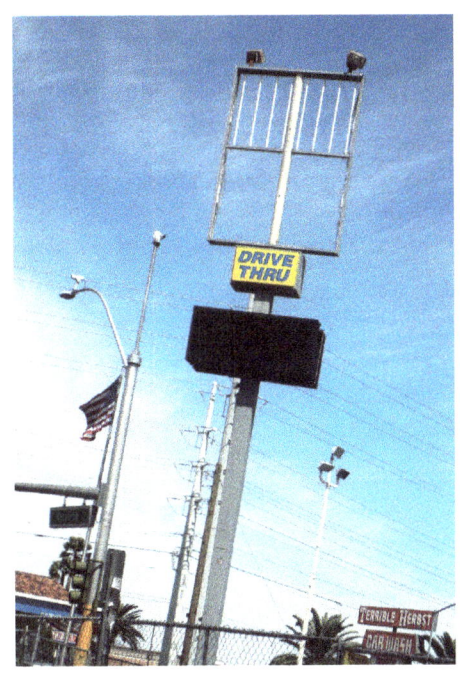

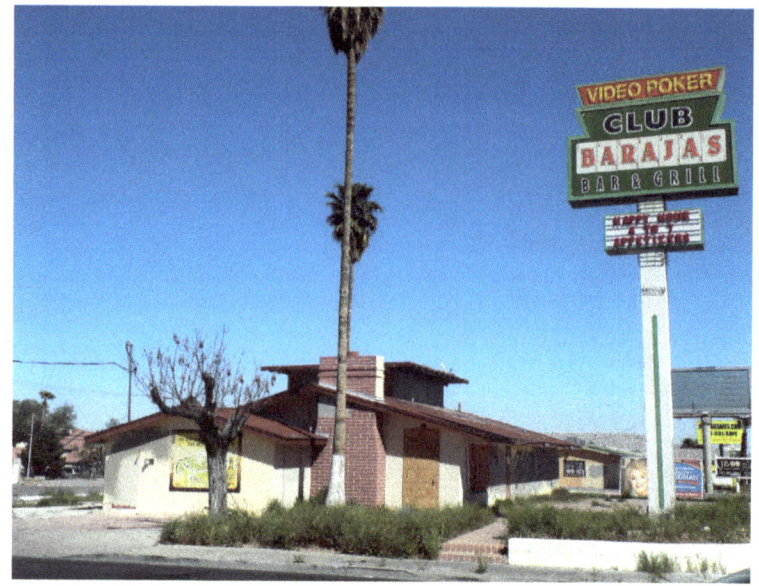

No more Happy Hour here. Since its closure in 2014, Club Barajas, located on Charleston Blvd., a few blocks east of Jones Blvd., now serves as a hotspot for homeless and taggers alike.

This Taco Bell at S. Maryland Parkway and Sahara Ave. closed down in April 2015. But, gordita fans, all is not lost, as a shiny, new Taco Bell replaces it just a few doors down on Maryland Pkwy. in summer 2015.

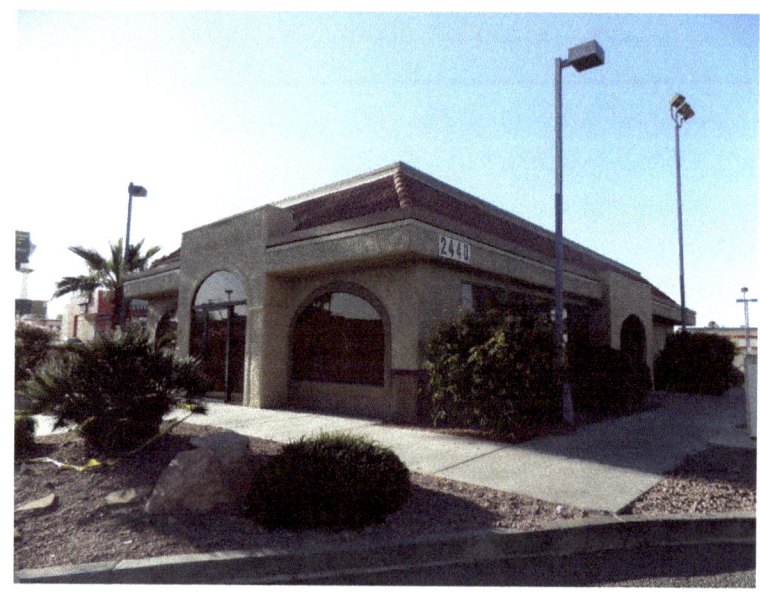

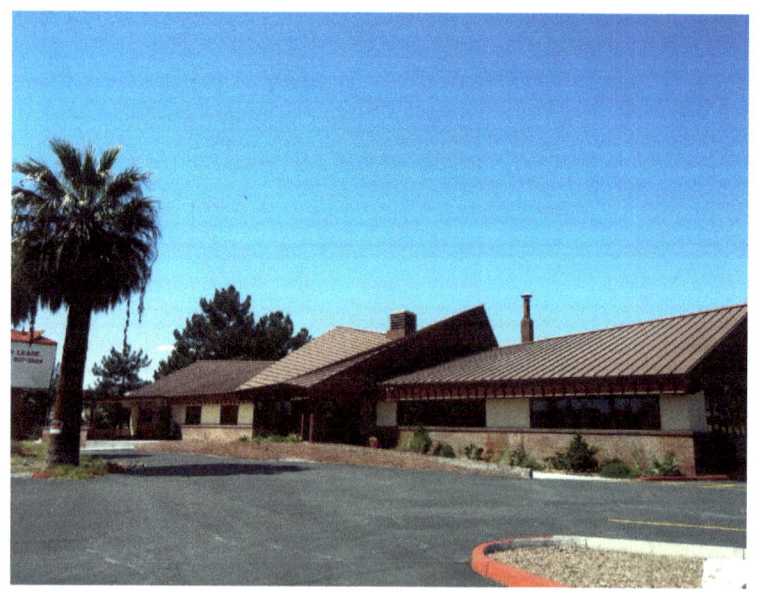

After sitting vacant for 5 years, there is finally hope for this location on Desert Inn Rd., just west of Eastern Ave. Over the years, it has seen many reincarnations: It has been a cowboy bar, a Mexican restaurant, a BBQ joint and an Asian buffet. In 2015, it re-opens as a Mexican restaurant once again.

# _making a withdrawal_

You know there's a problem when one of the largest financial institutions in town closes shop. In late 2014, Citigroup closed its sprawling 120,000-square-foot facility on W. Sahara Ave., west of Durango Dr. In the early '80s, Citicorp (as it was known then) first opened the $8 million credit-card processing center with 1,000 employees.

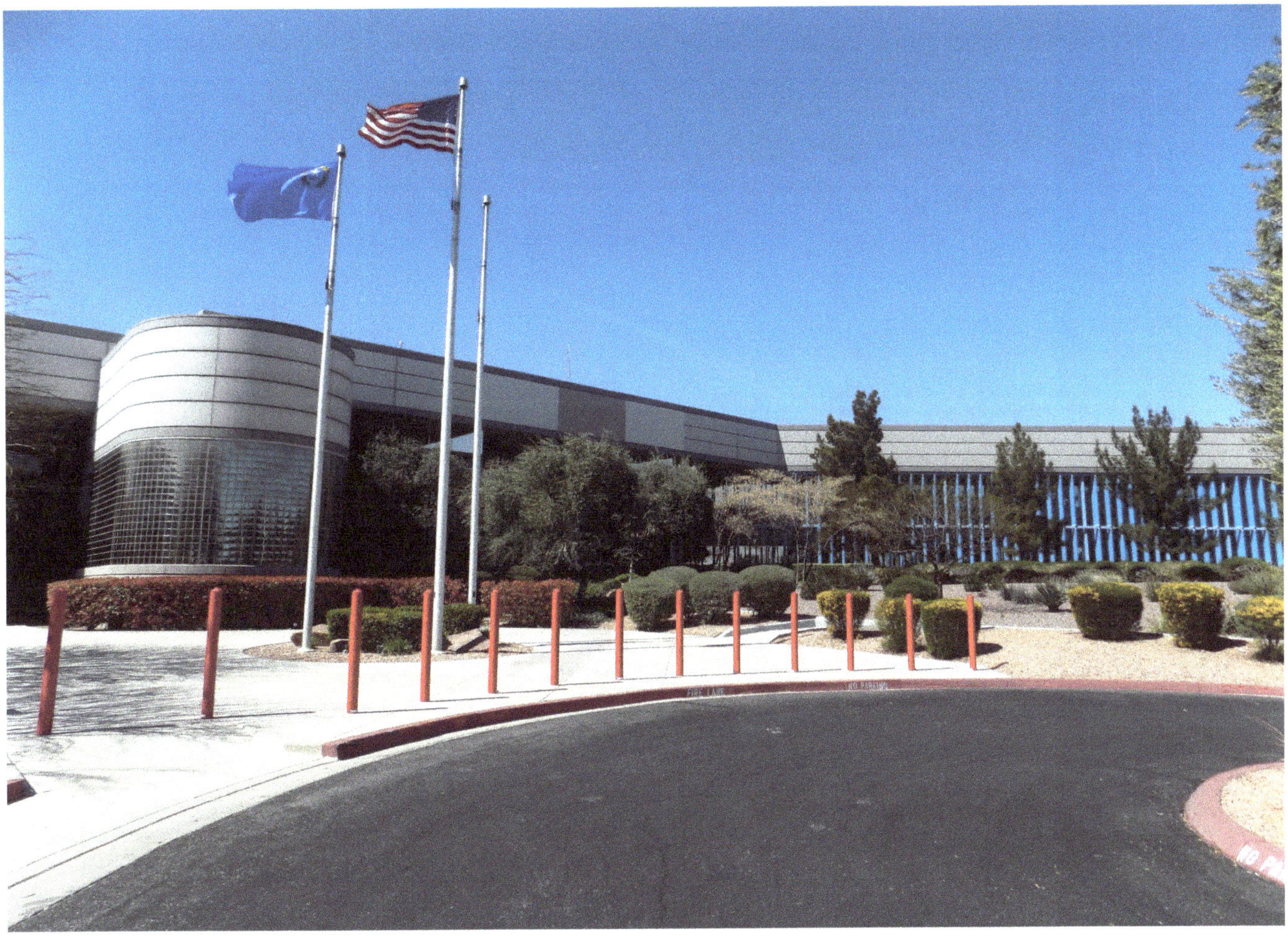

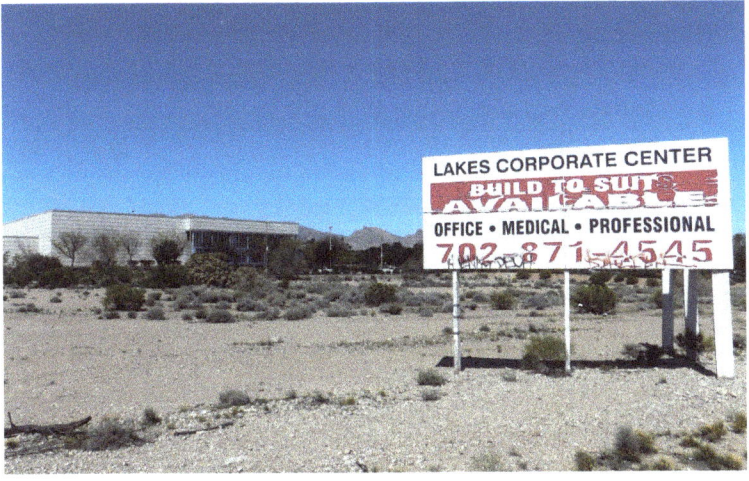

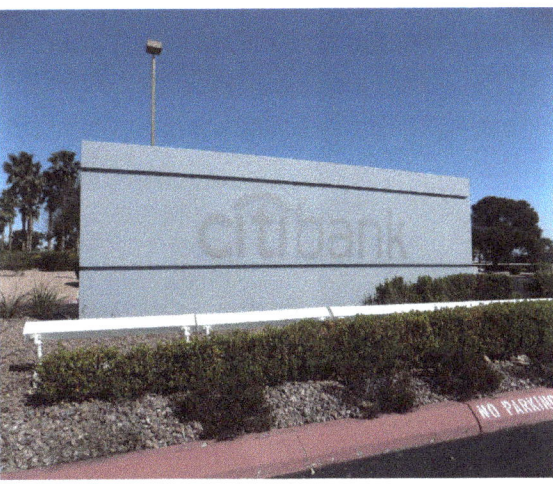

# *dried up*

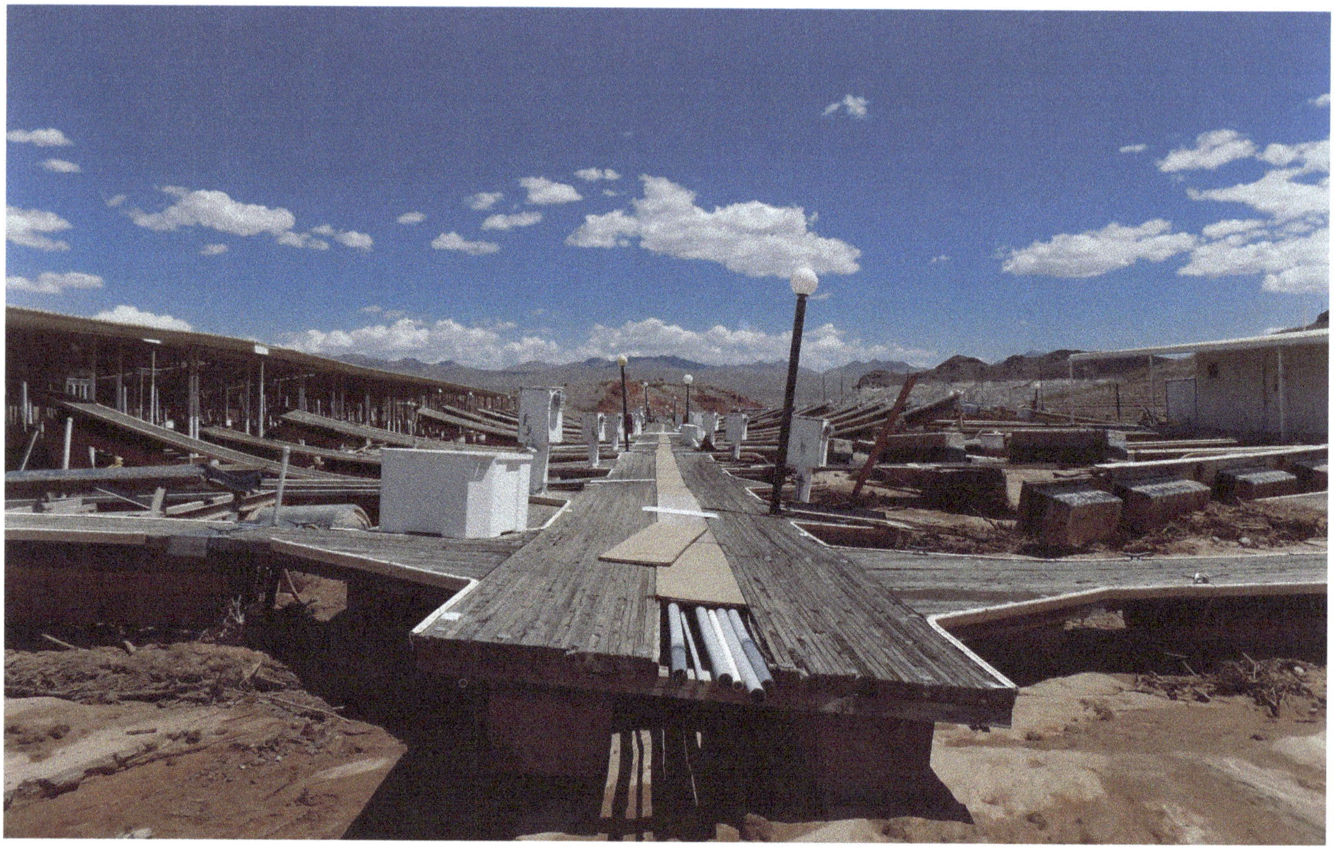

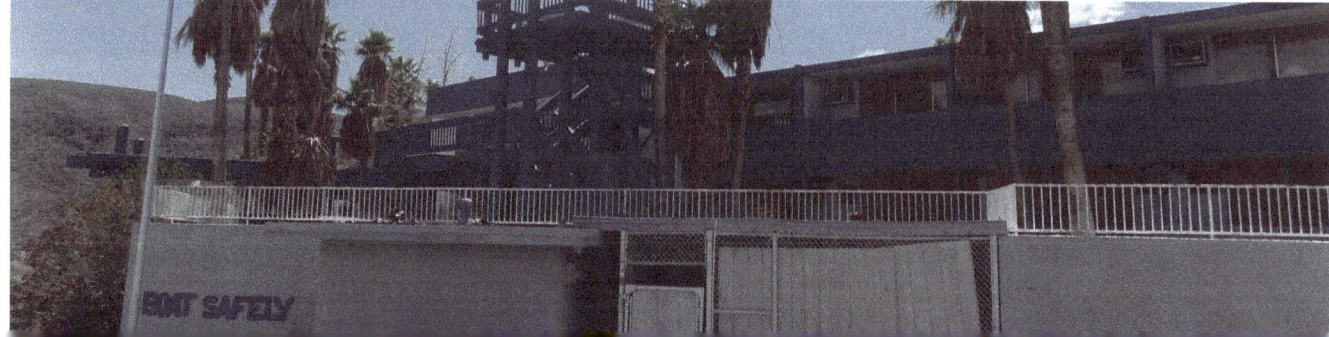

Lake Mead's Echo Bay Marina was shut down in February 2013. Forever Resorts, which ran the facility, reached the end of their contract in January 2013. When it came time to find a new operator, the National Park Service didn't receive any bids for the next 10-year contract.

Echo Bay Marina had become too costly to operate, due to the lack of boat slip rentals and the drop in water levels at the lake. The marina's small motel and restaurant both closed in 2010 due to dwindling revenues during the Recession. Currently, they sit boarded up, left behind along with the abandoned marine fueling station and 365 slips that have been ravaged by the desert sun.

A year after the marina's closure, Lake Mead had dropped to its lowest level since first filled in the 1930s (upon the completion of the Hoover Dam). 14 years of drought had forced waters down more than 130 feet since a high-water mark was last reached in 2000, leaving North America's largest man-made reservoir just 39 percent full.

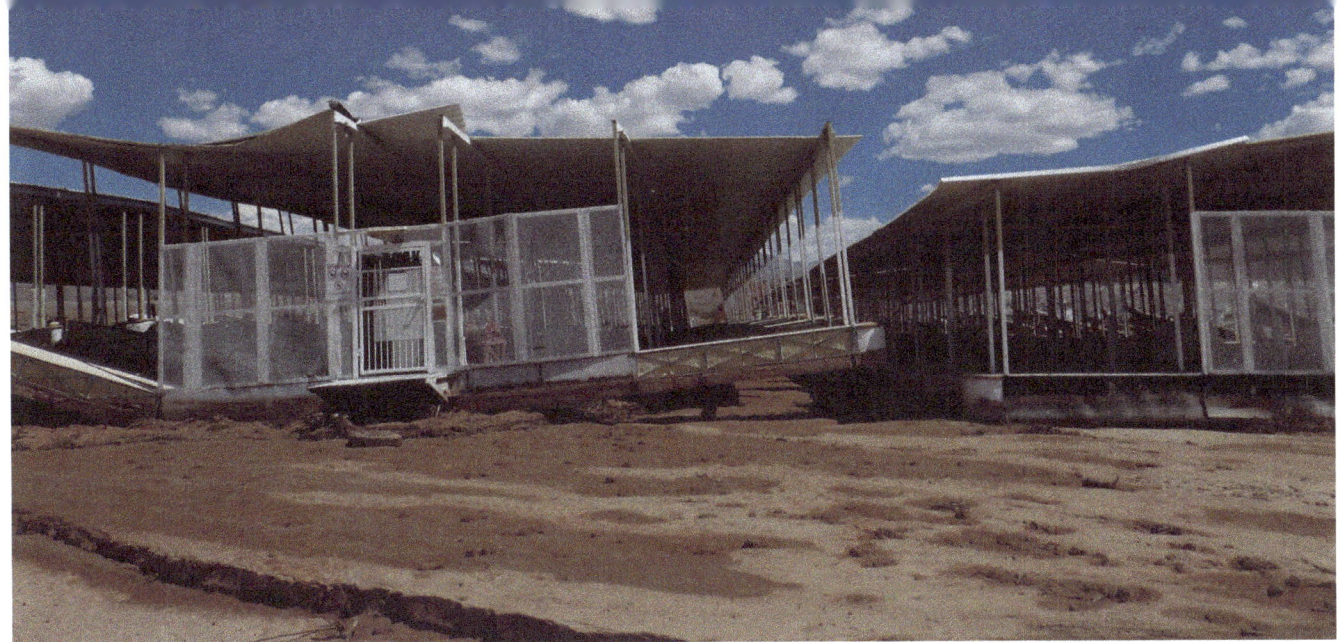

It's an eerie feeling walking the few hundred yards from the now-defunct boat launch to the desolate marina along ground formerly underwater. The landscape, shaped by water ripples and waves, is now exposed and has cracked under the blistering desert sun.

The unstable facility has begun to buckle and break apart. The warping dock has cracked, forcing sections of it upward, while other segments swallowed by sand succumb to the desert's relentless appetite. Its windows broken out, the marina shop is left barren. The land is littered with trash and debris revealed by evaporating waters and left behind in the wake of the marina's demise.

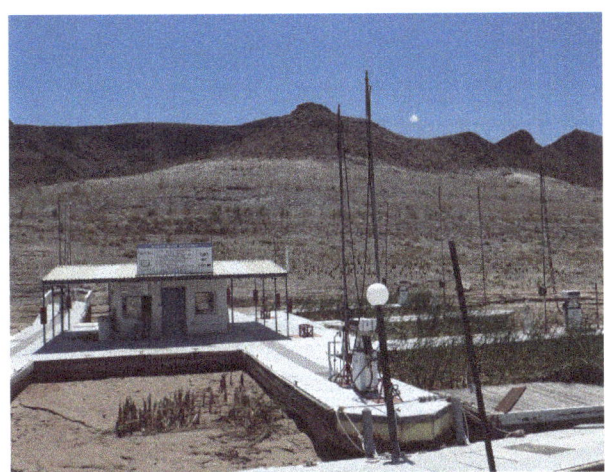

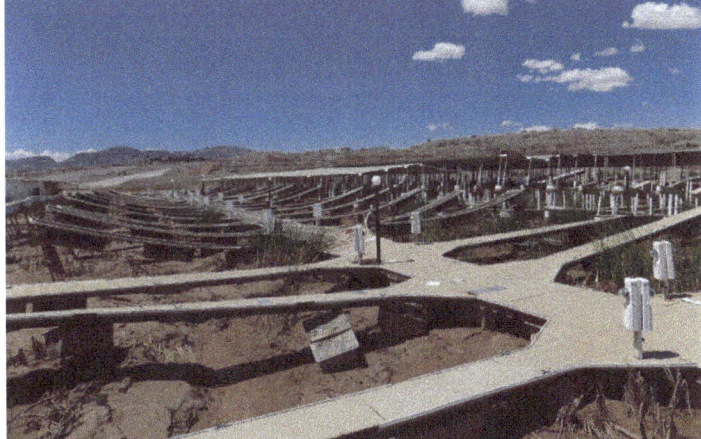

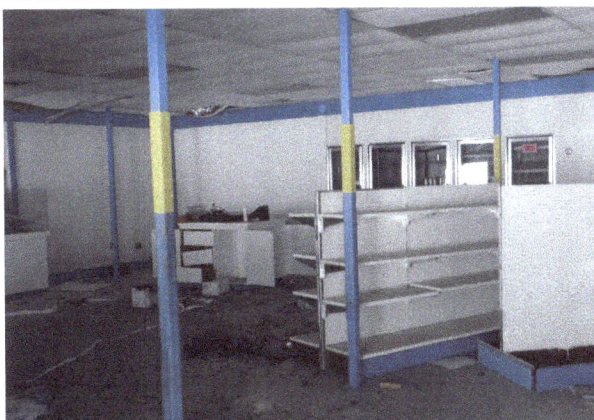

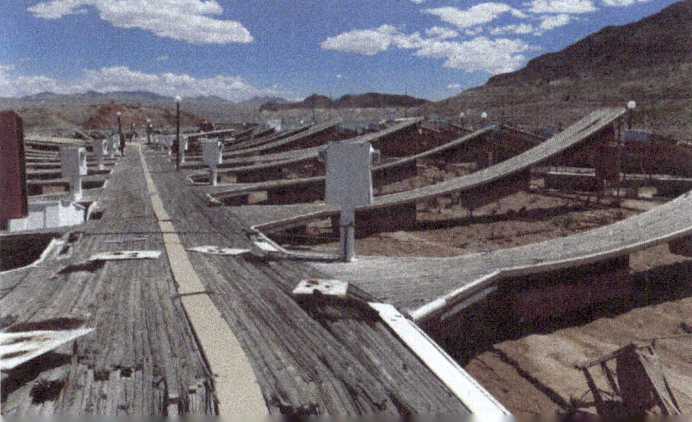

# the house always wins?

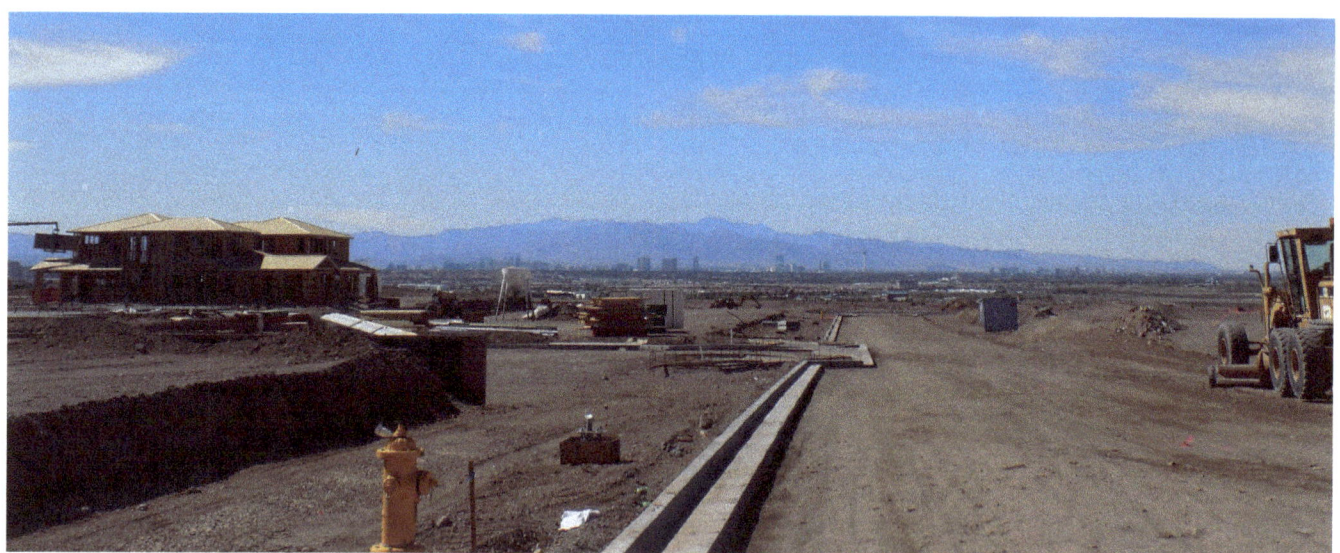

Hit hard by the housing crisis, Las Vegas has been slow to recover. But there is hope. Pictured above, after years dormant, construction has once again started at master planned community Cadence in Henderson.

While there may be some truth to that commonly heard phrase "The house always wins" at the casinos, it definitely isn't always the case once you head off-Strip into residential Las Vegas. It's no secret that the housing bust is at the root of much of Las Vegas' hardship. When the market crashed in 2008, the housing boom came to an end. Left in its wake were hundreds of stalled developments and the loss of thousands of jobs.

In the years following the crash, Nevada had the highest foreclosure rate in the country, and Vegas was frequently listed as one of the top 5 cities with the most foreclosures. When the economy went belly up, people were losing their jobs, and many could no longer afford their homes. So as people were forced to move out, banks repossessed these homes.

The Vegas housing inventory was massively increasing as banks worked feverishly to get these foreclosed homes back on the market at low, low prices, hoping to try and recoup their losses. What ended up happening is that Vegas was left with a glut of houses, a sea of inventory, vacant and ready to be occupied. But as jobs were dying, people couldn't afford to buy. And as many developers declared bankruptcy, those remaining found it difficult to compete with the existing homes being sold off by banks at discount prices. As a result, many of the new housing projects stalled. Less buyers, more houses, crisis.

To move these newer homes, they, too, were being offered at bargain-basement prices. This put older Vegas, east of the I-15, into a precarious position, which makes sense. Buy a newer home in a shinier, cleaner, safer part of town for less than what the older part of town cost just a few years prior? The decision seems easy. So for the people who were still buying, they were opting for newer parts of town, west of the I-15. Older Vegas took a hit, as evidenced throughout this book. Less people in the neighborhood, no need for two Albertsons a few blocks apart. With store closures comes more job loss. With vacant buildings comes more homeless people and crime.

As someone who has been studying the Vegas market aggressively since 2011, as of 2015, I can tell you there has been an improvement. The neighborhoods I was eyeing in 2011 are now offering homes, on average, for about 30% higher asking prices than they were four years ago. But while that is promising, the stats are telling us Las Vegas is nowhere near rebounding to what it was in its boom days, and foreclosures are still most definitely a problem.

According to a report from RealtyTrac released in March 2015, Nevada had the second-highest foreclosure rate in the country, with one in 569 homes receiving a foreclosure filing. The Silver State comes in second only to Maryland, which had one in 564 homes with a foreclosure filing.

For Nevada, it's a step in the wrong direction. One year prior, the report from RealtyTrac listed Nevada as the state with the third-highest foreclosure rate, with one in 633 houses receiving a foreclosure-related filing. At the time, only Maryland and Florida had higher foreclosure rates.

At the end of 2014, 88,037 Las Vegas-area homeowners were underwater. That's an estimated 26.4 percent of Southern Nevada homeowners. The upside is that it's an improvement, down from 35.1 percent of homeowners underwater a year prior, and well below its peak of 71 percent in the first quarter of 2012.

What's all this mean for Vegas? There is hope. Slowly but surely, long-stalled projects are firing up once again. I see it all over town. Housing developments that have been sitting dormant for the last few years are finally now seeing some action. So while the city is surely not rebounding as quickly as many other metropolitan areas, it is recovering. Las Vegas, once the fastest-growing major city in America, will once again have its day. It won't be this year, and it likely won't even be next year, but it will happen again.

Considering Las Vegas' past as one of the most hotly sought-after U.S. cities for home owners and investors, in time, the future can only be brighter. Vegas is coming back.

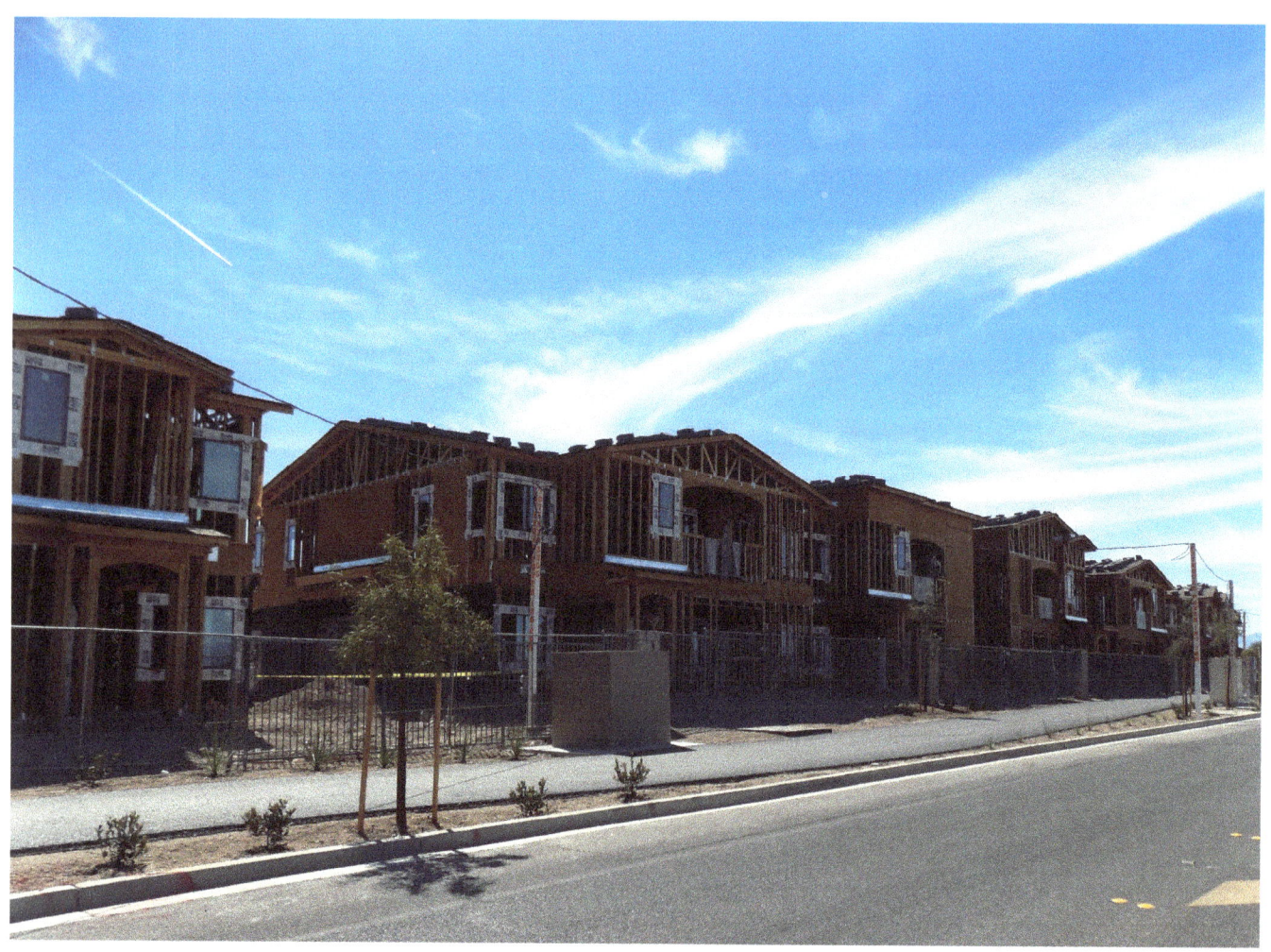

Henderson is one of the nicest areas to live in the Vegas metro area. Essentially a suburb, it's located just south of McCarran Airport and is a relatively short drive to the Strip. Much of the area first developed in the '90s and 2000s. And for being east of the I-15, which is typically considered "older" Vegas, it is surely the cleanest, newest and safest area on that side of the interstate.

In December 2014, real estate blog Movoto named Henderson, NV, the fifth safest big city in the country. Survey was based on FBI stats and census data. Irvine, CA, topped the list of safest cities, followed by Fremont, CA, Gilbert, AZ, and Plano, TX.

Signs of hope are seen throughout Henderson, as shown in these shots of various housing developments that are either beginning new construction or had stalled out during the Recession and are now coming back to life. (Photos: This page, new housing development at Wigwam Pkwy. and Gibson Rd.; Opposite page, construction continues on new homes off Horizon Ridge Pkwy., just east of Gibson Rd.)

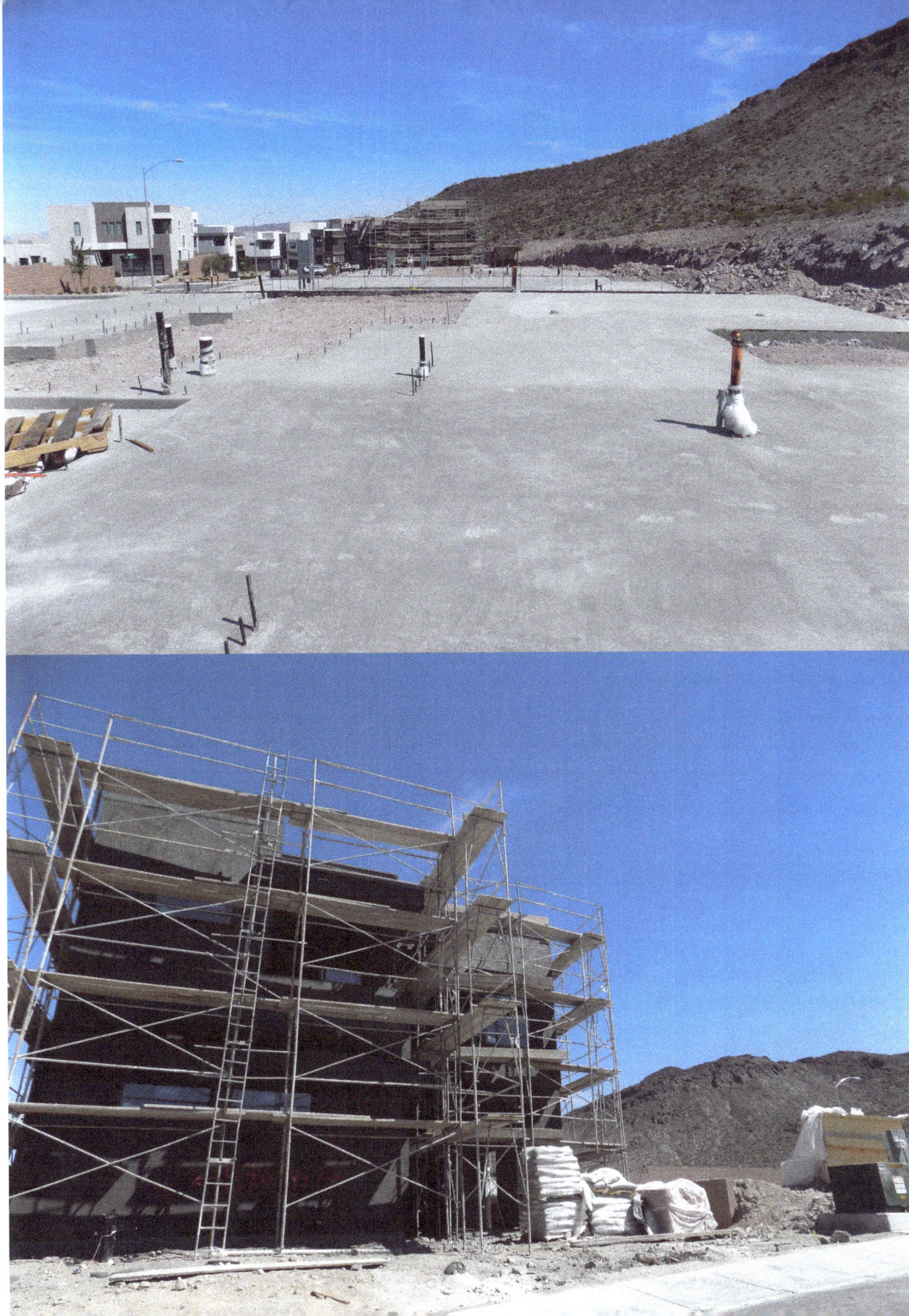

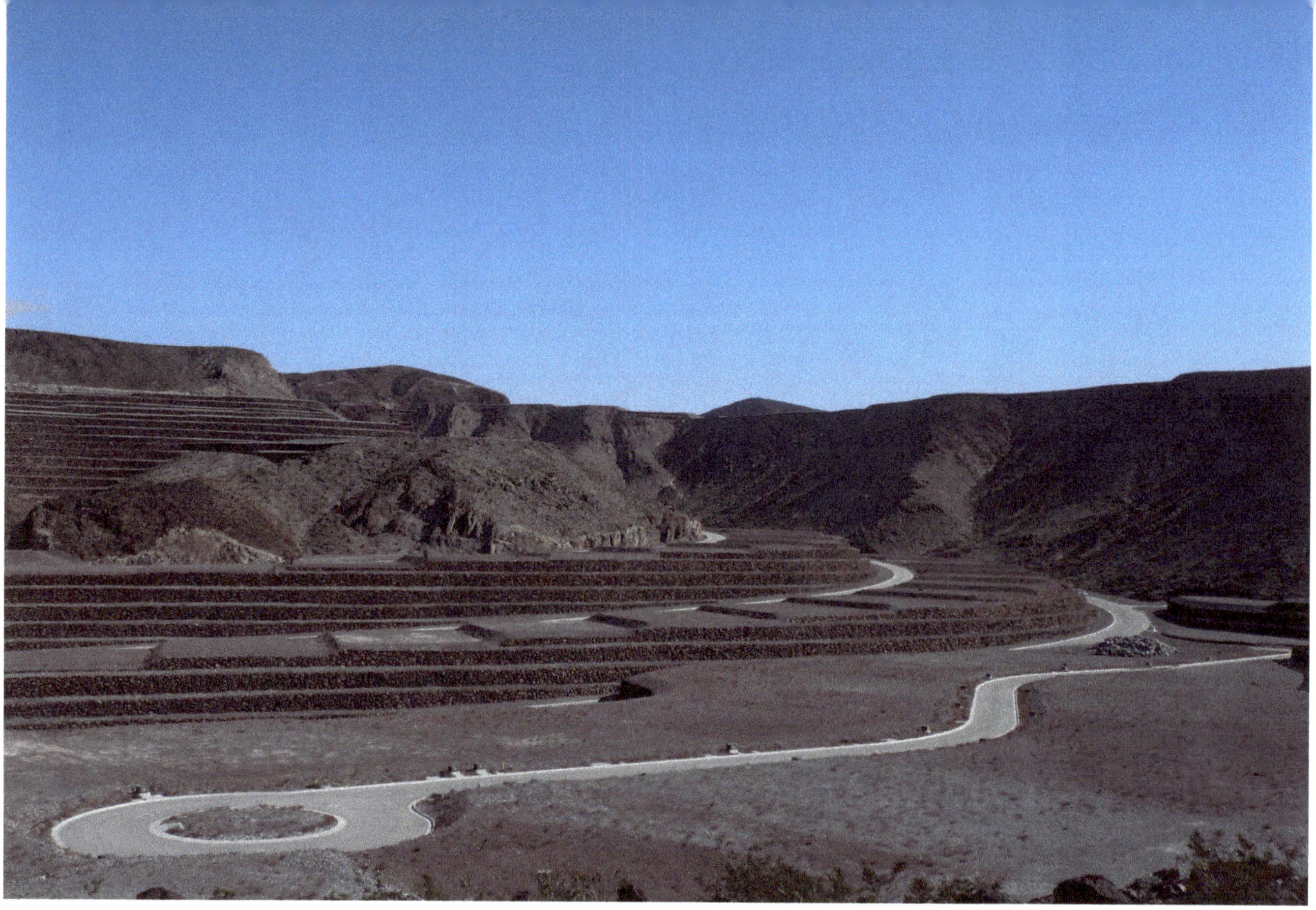

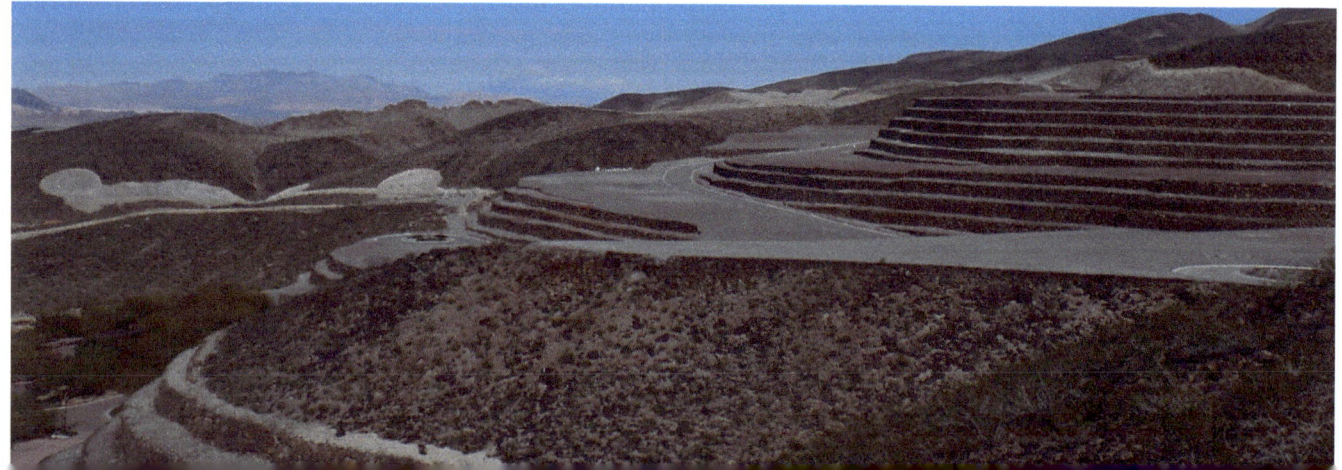

Developed by Hong Kong tycoon Henry Cheng, the upscale residential community Ascaya, located in Henderson, stalled out in 2009. The lots are graded, the roads built, and underground utilities have been installed. But as of 2015, the luxury neighborhood up on the mountainside, with stellar views of the Strip, doesn't have a single home. But there is hope.

Located almost 1,000 feet above the valley floor in the McCullough Range, walking the desolate terrain of Ascaya feels like being on another planet, a lost world long since deserted. Of course, the reality is that Ascaya has yet to be inhabited - but that looks to be changing. In October 2014, Ascaya developers sold their first lot (a 0.46-acre parcel) for $925,000.

Management now aims to sell the 313 lots in phases and hopes to have the project fully developed within a decade.

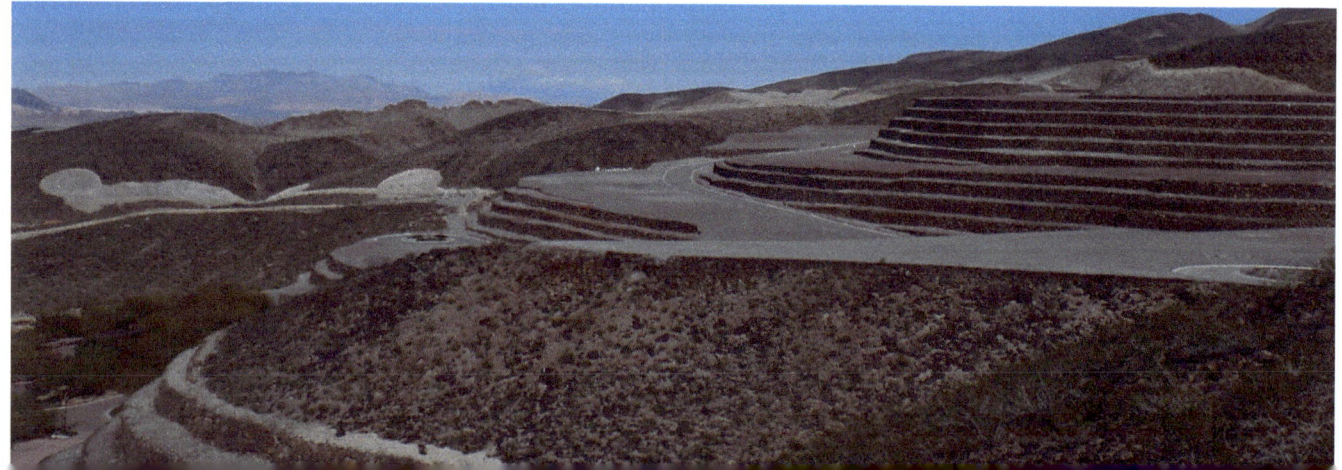

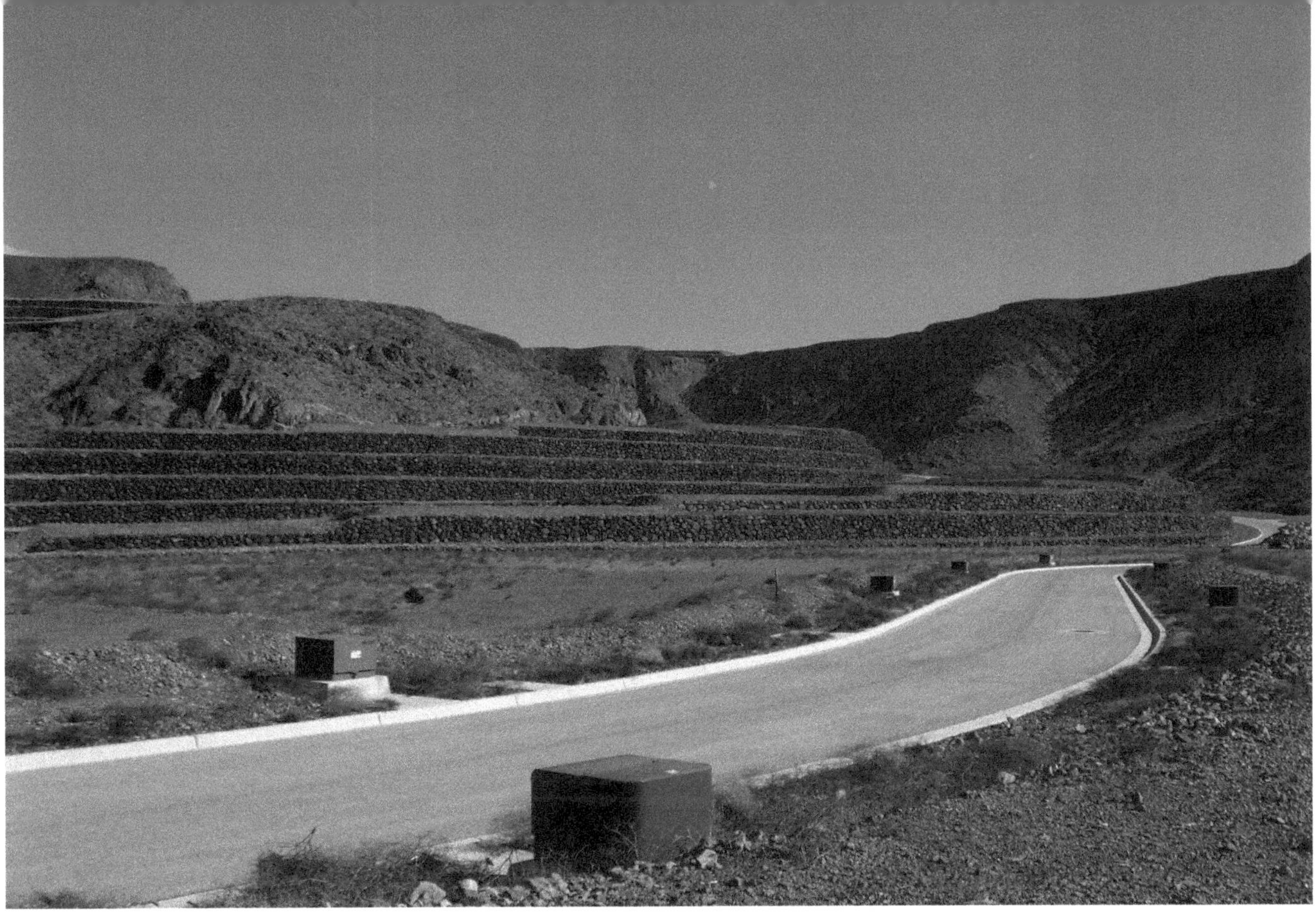

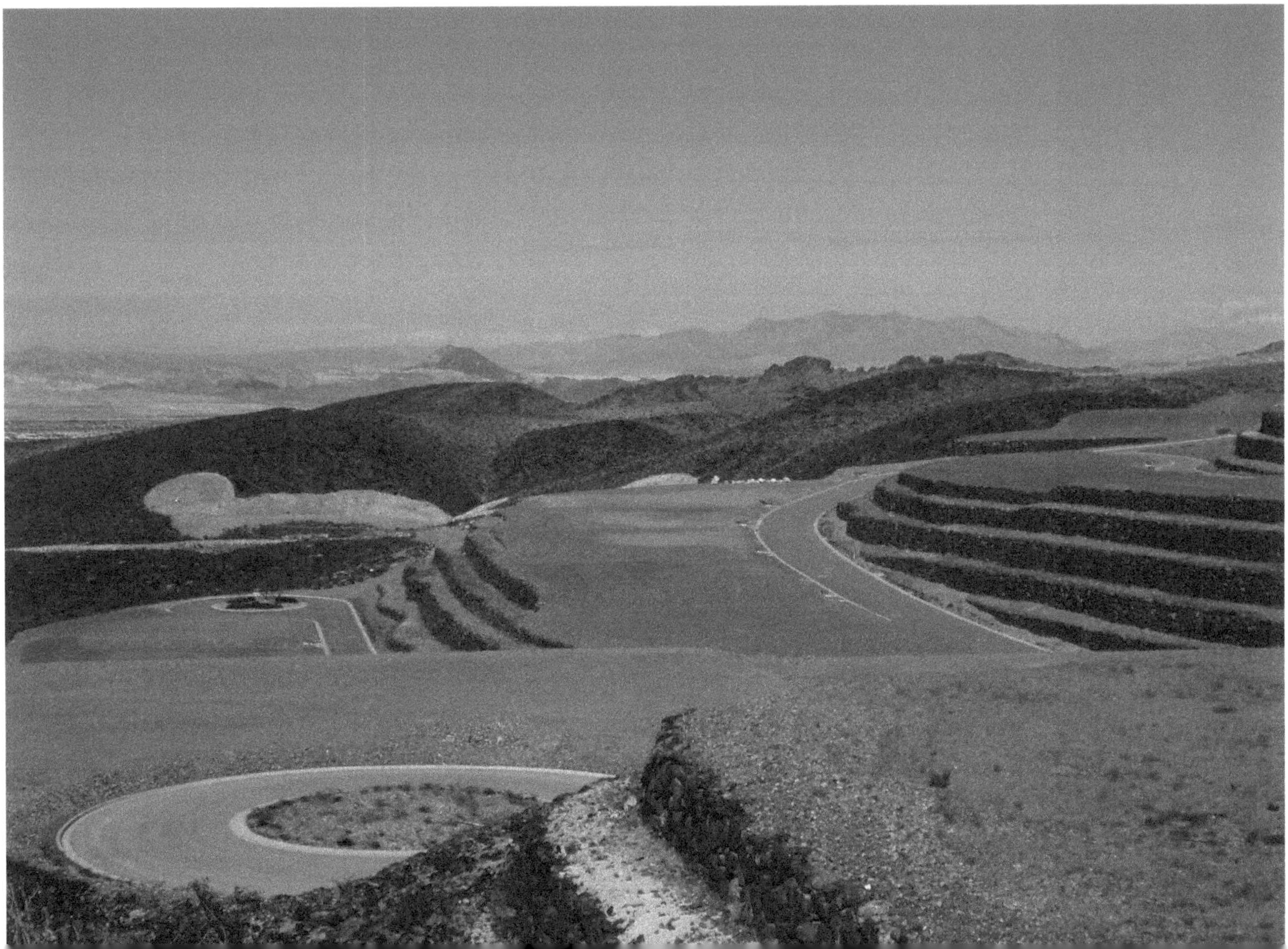

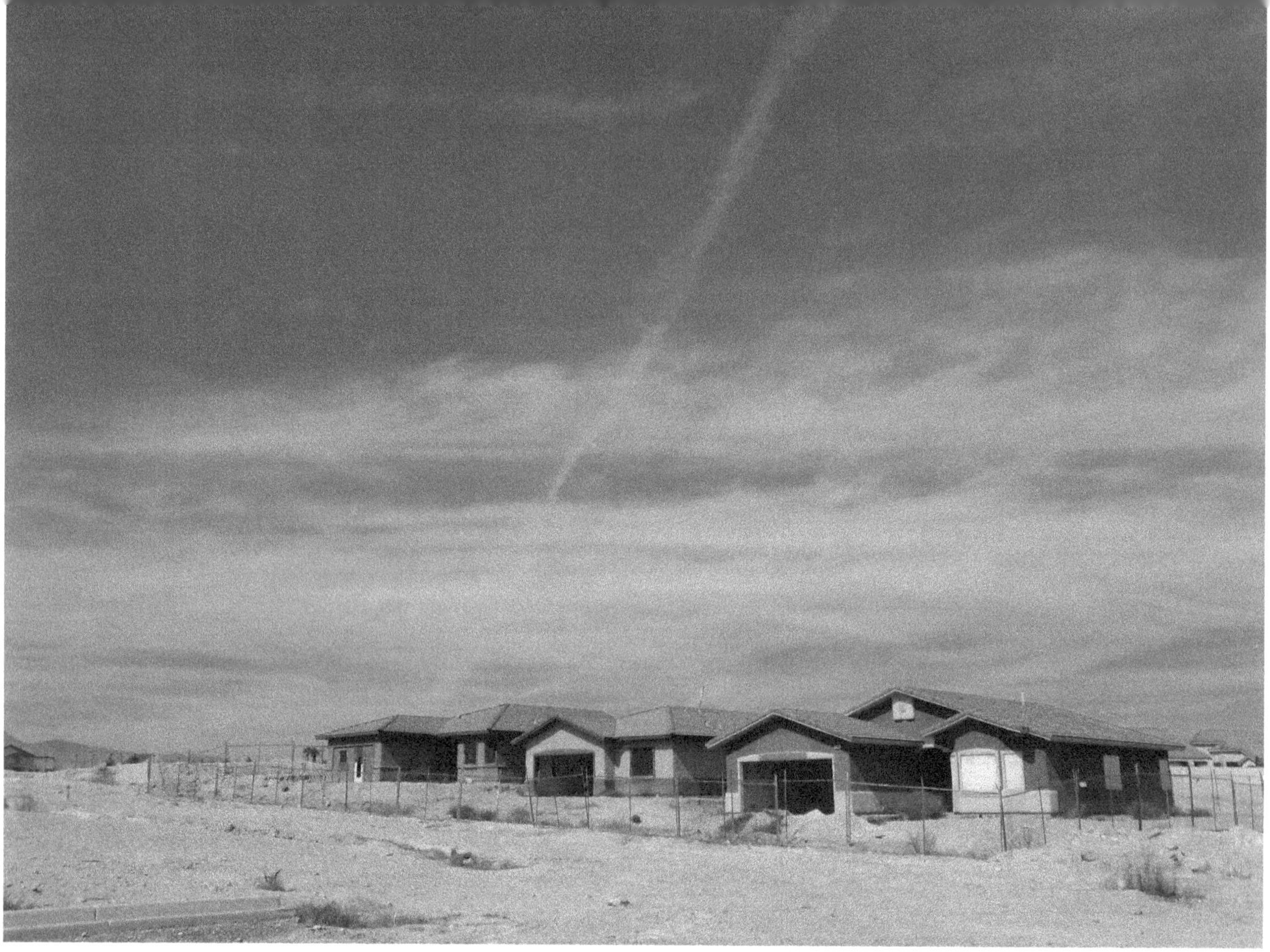

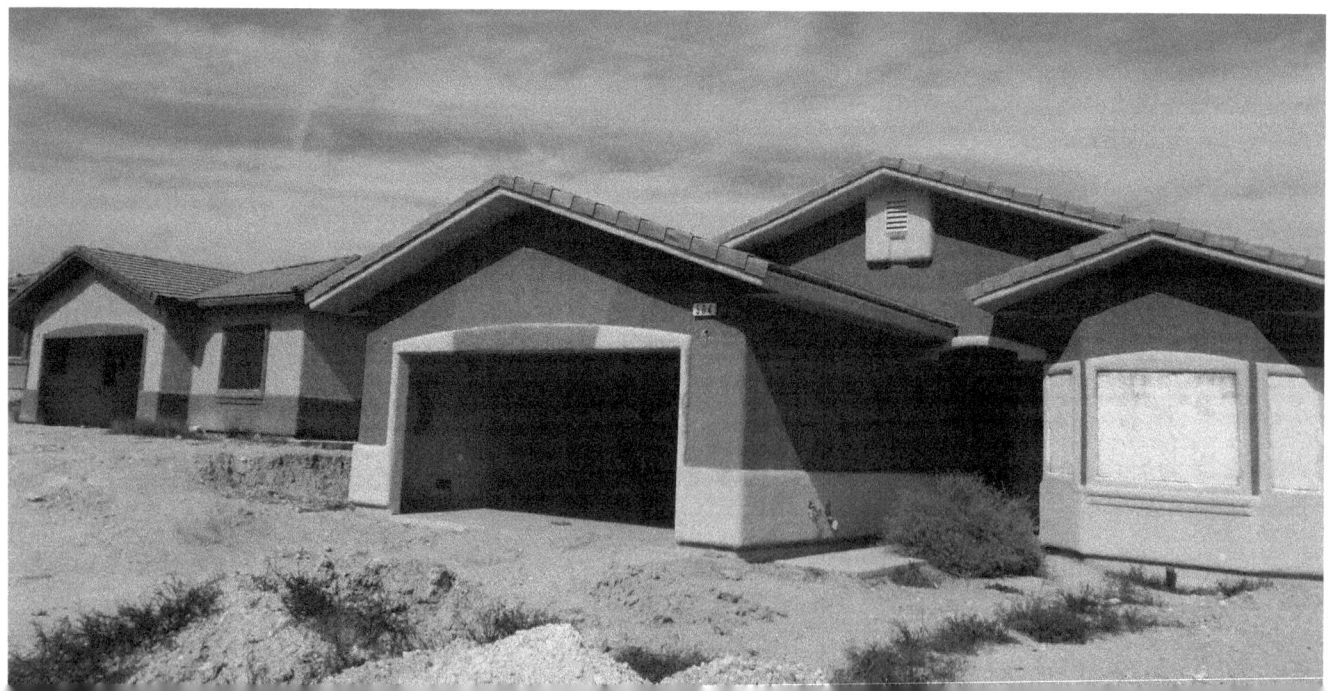

The Desert Mesa project, located in North Las Vegas at Carey Avenue near Commerce Street, was envisioned as a residential development for low-income families. Its development was slowed by construction delays, lawsuits from contractors and soil problems. Financial hardship brought on by the Recession has left the community vacant for over 10 years, as construction halted in 2004.

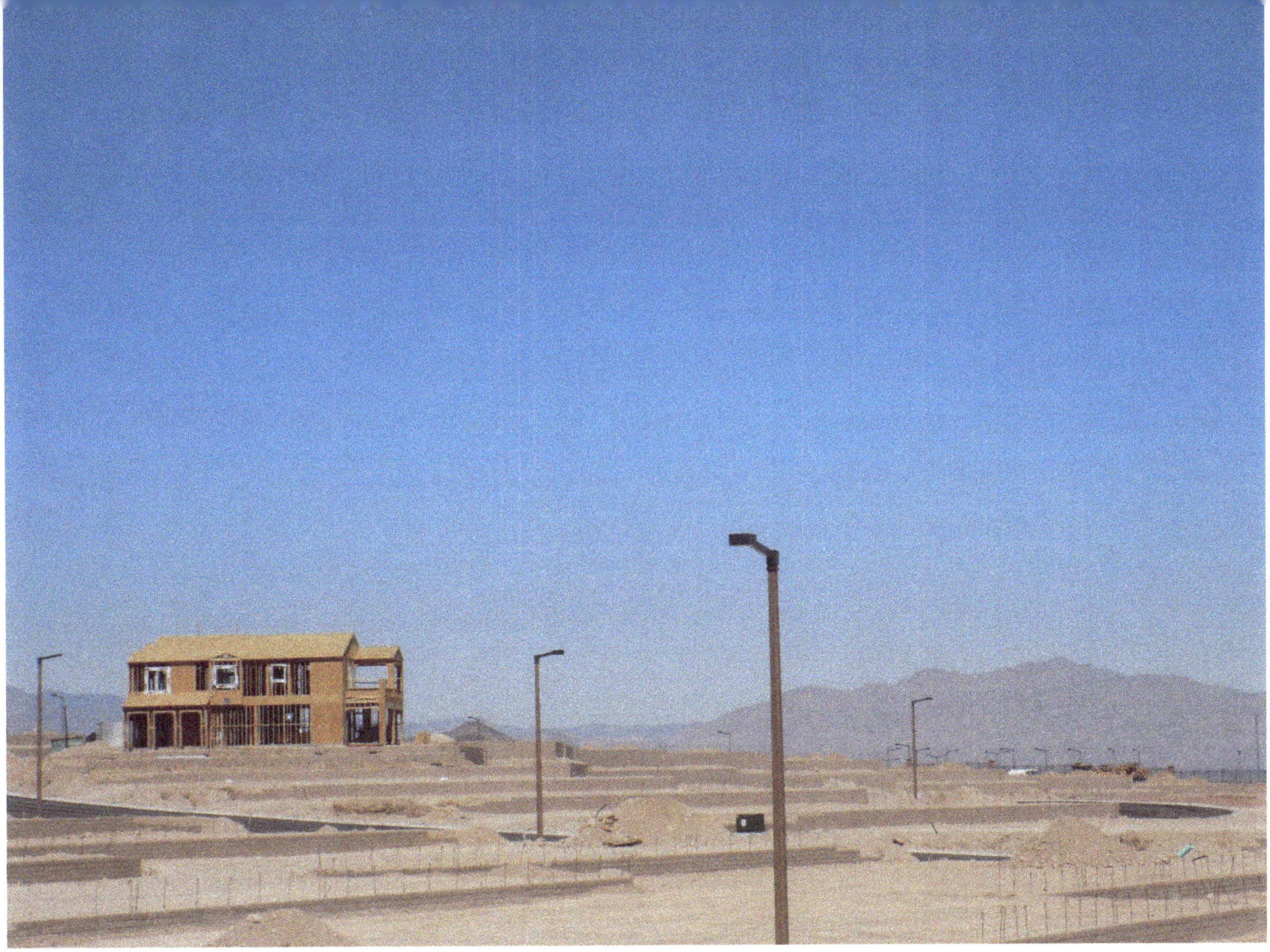

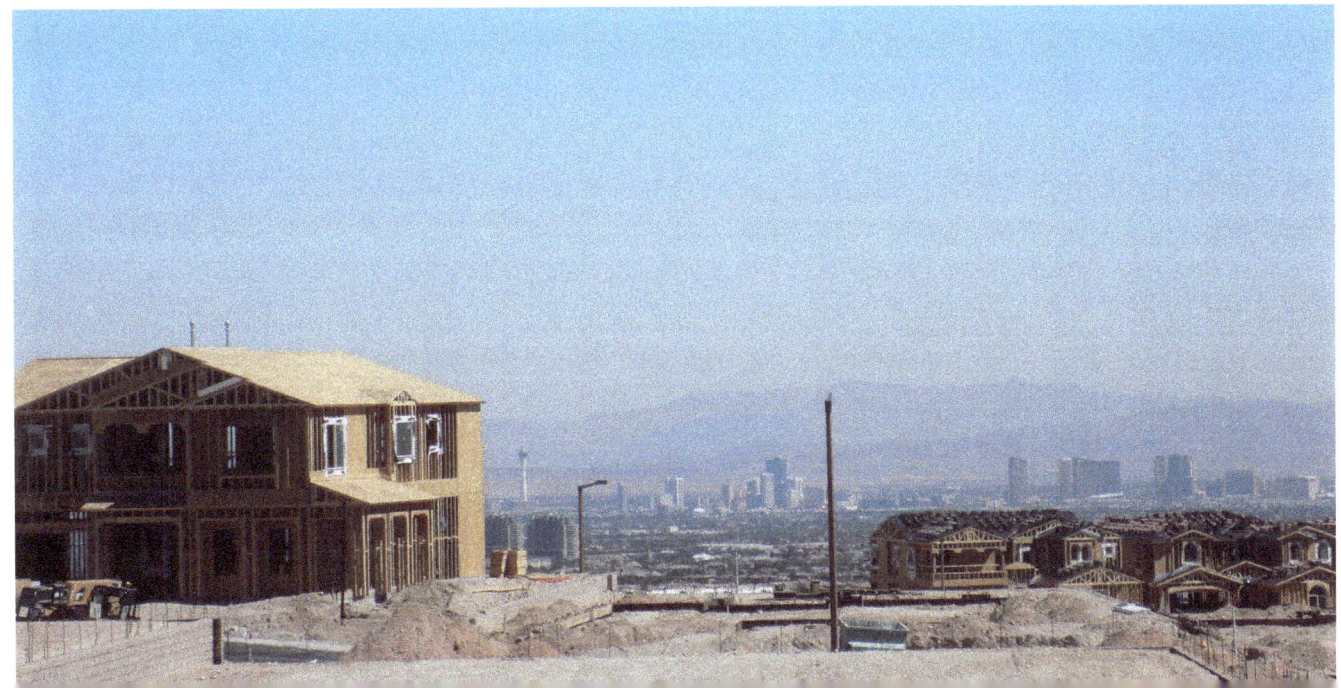

The affluent suburb of Summerlin, located approximately 25 minutes west of the Strip, wasn't immune to the Recession. The majestic Red Rock Canyon serves as a backdrop to the master planned community, developed mostly in the '90s and 2000s. Nestled alongside the mountains, Summerlin offers breathtaking views of the Strip. While many housing developments had stalled out, Summerlin is most definitely seeing construction activity once again.

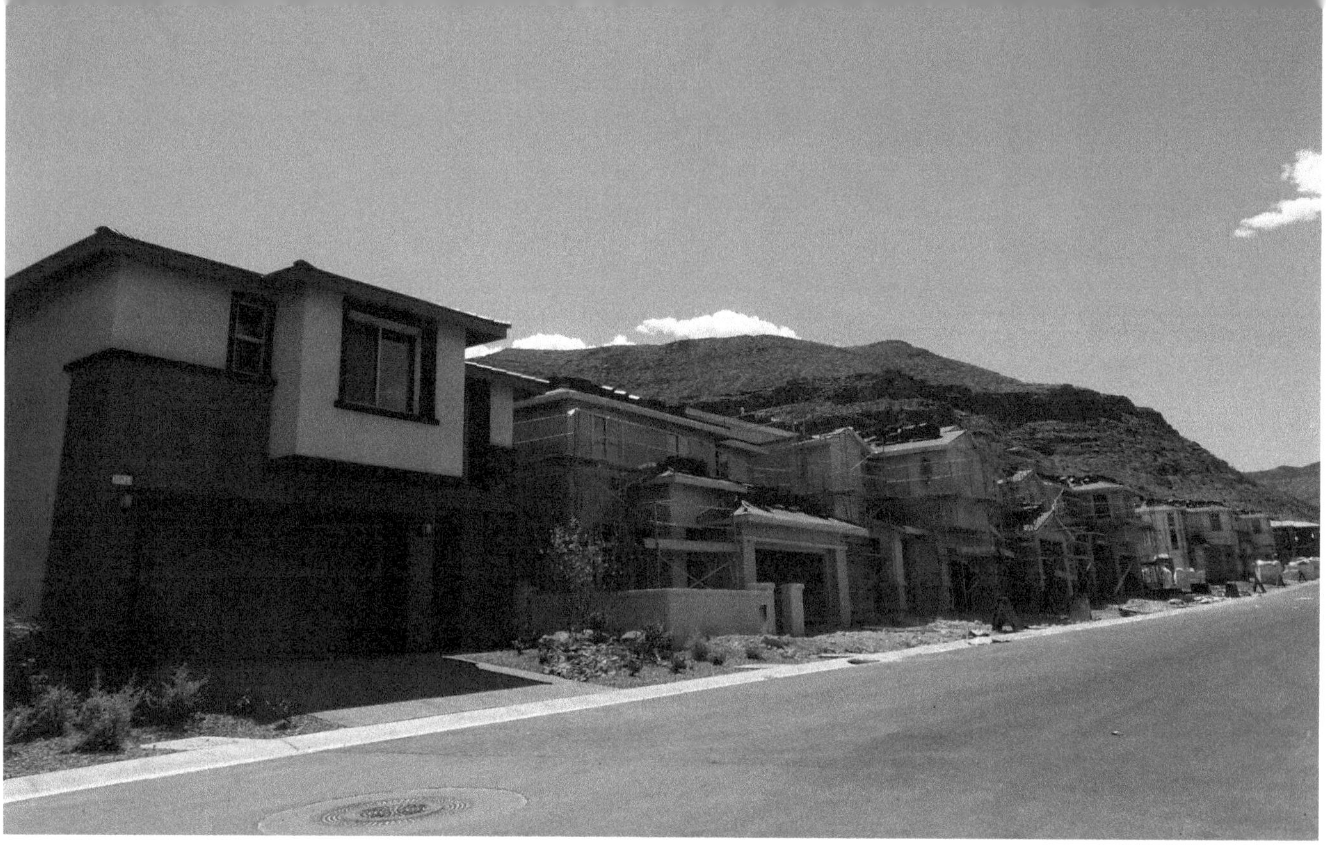

**Above:** One down...a few more to go! Located in the Summerlin village of the Mesa, the neighborhood Cielo is still under construction. Homebuilder Woodside Homes re-emerged in 2010 after two years in bankruptcy.

**Below:** All that's missing from this gorgeous neighborhood street in Cielo are neighbors chatting and kids playing outside. Currently, only one house on this street is occupied.

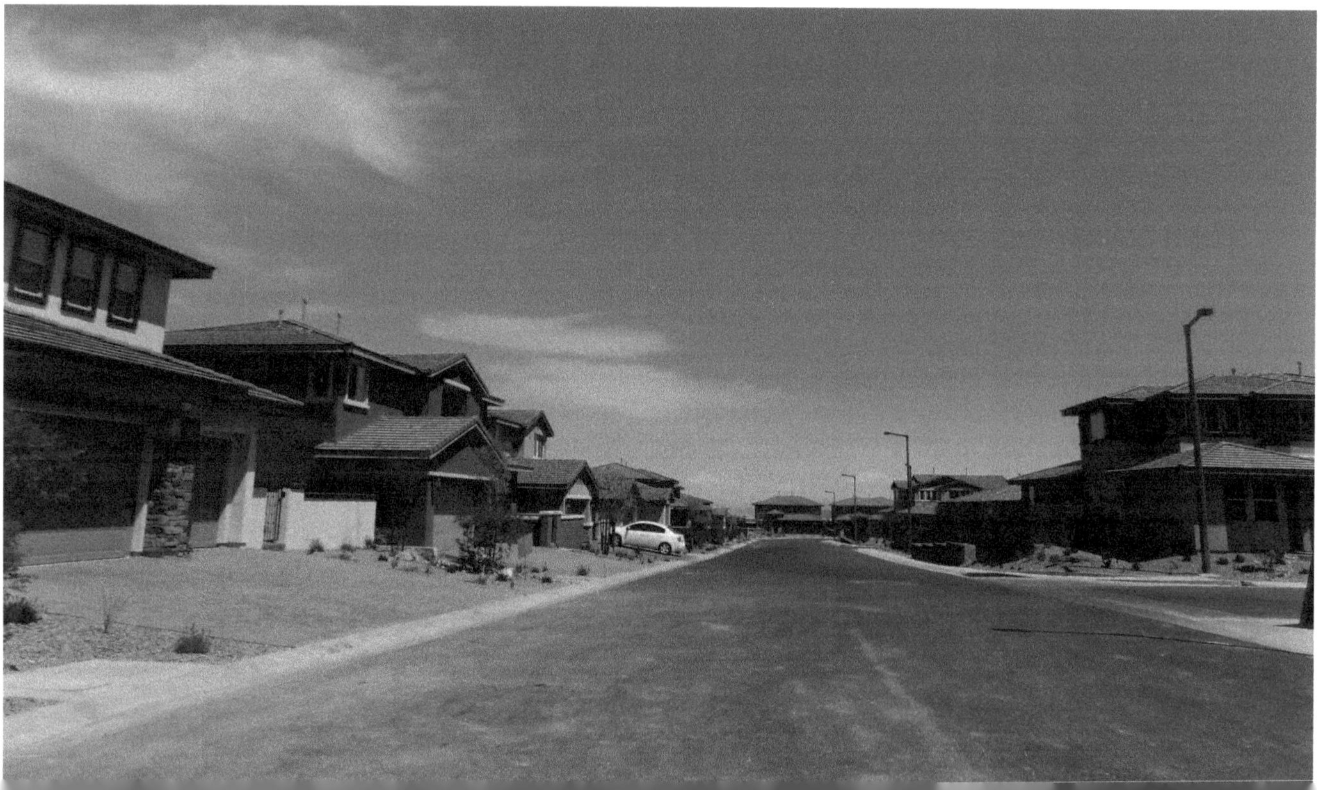

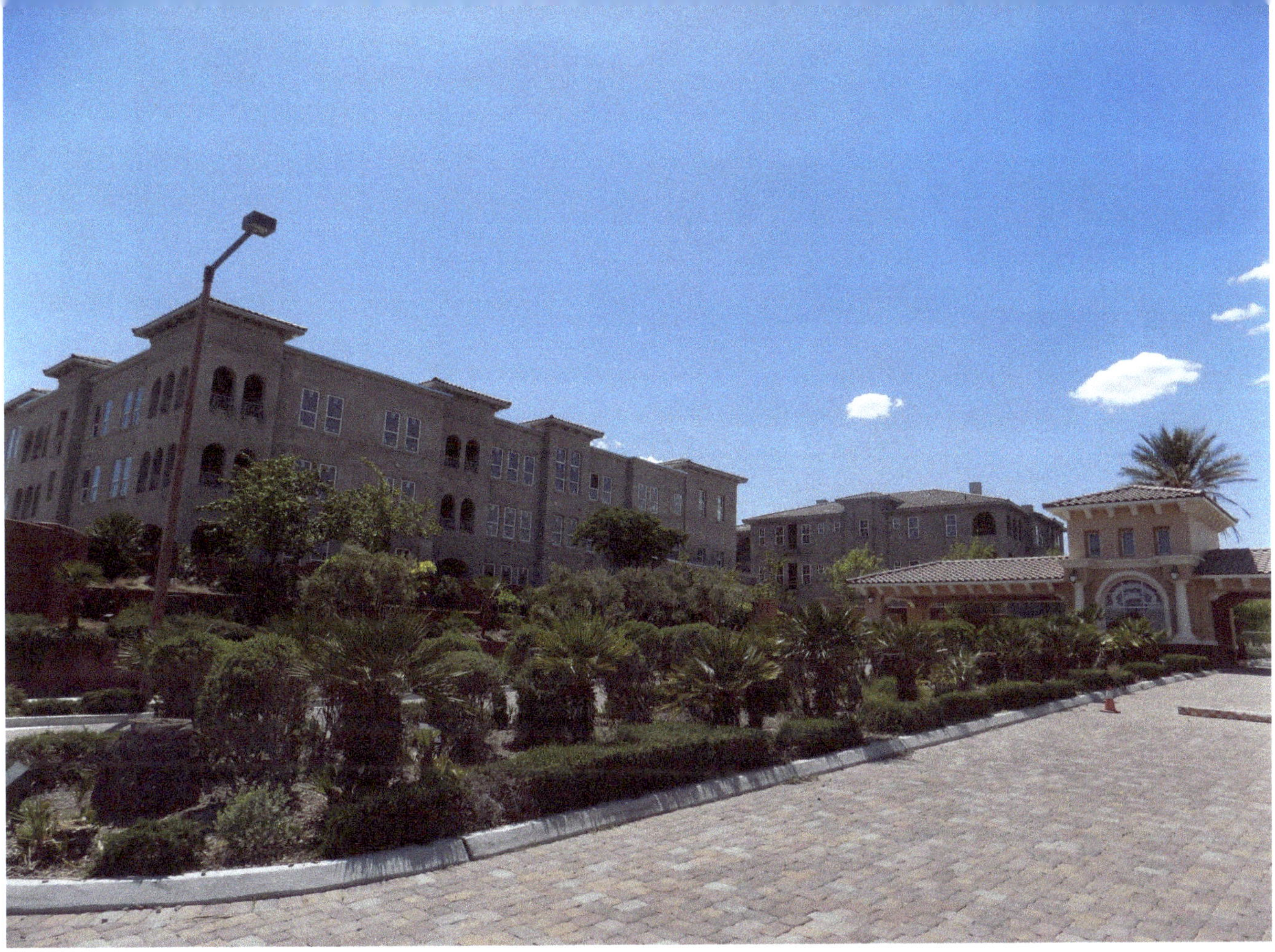

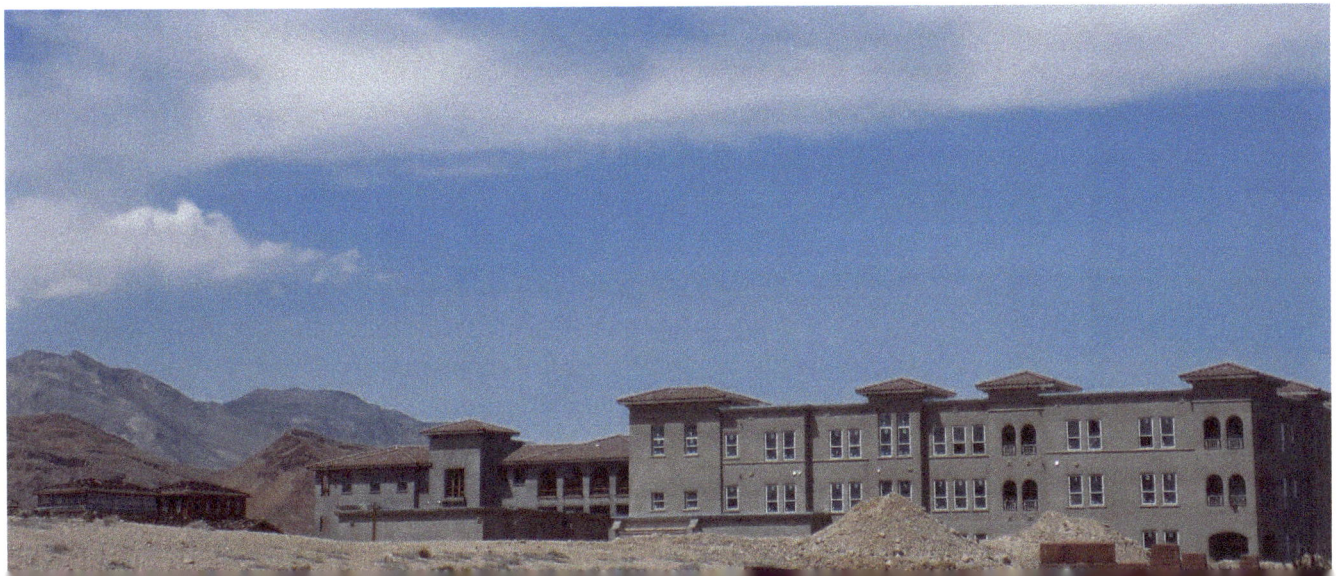

Beautiful and lonely, what was to be the high-end, age-qualified neighborhood Montechiaro in Summerlin has been sitting vacant since 2008, when developer Westmark Homes filed for bankruptcy. Only a few of the buildings, seen here, were built, originally intended as part of a massive complex, which was to include an array of amenities and resort-style living for active adults. Located on 50-plus acres at the southwest corner of Flamingo Road and Town Center Drive, the mid-rise neighborhood was to offer housing options starting in the low $300s. No plans have been announced for the property, which has been sitting unfinished for seven years.

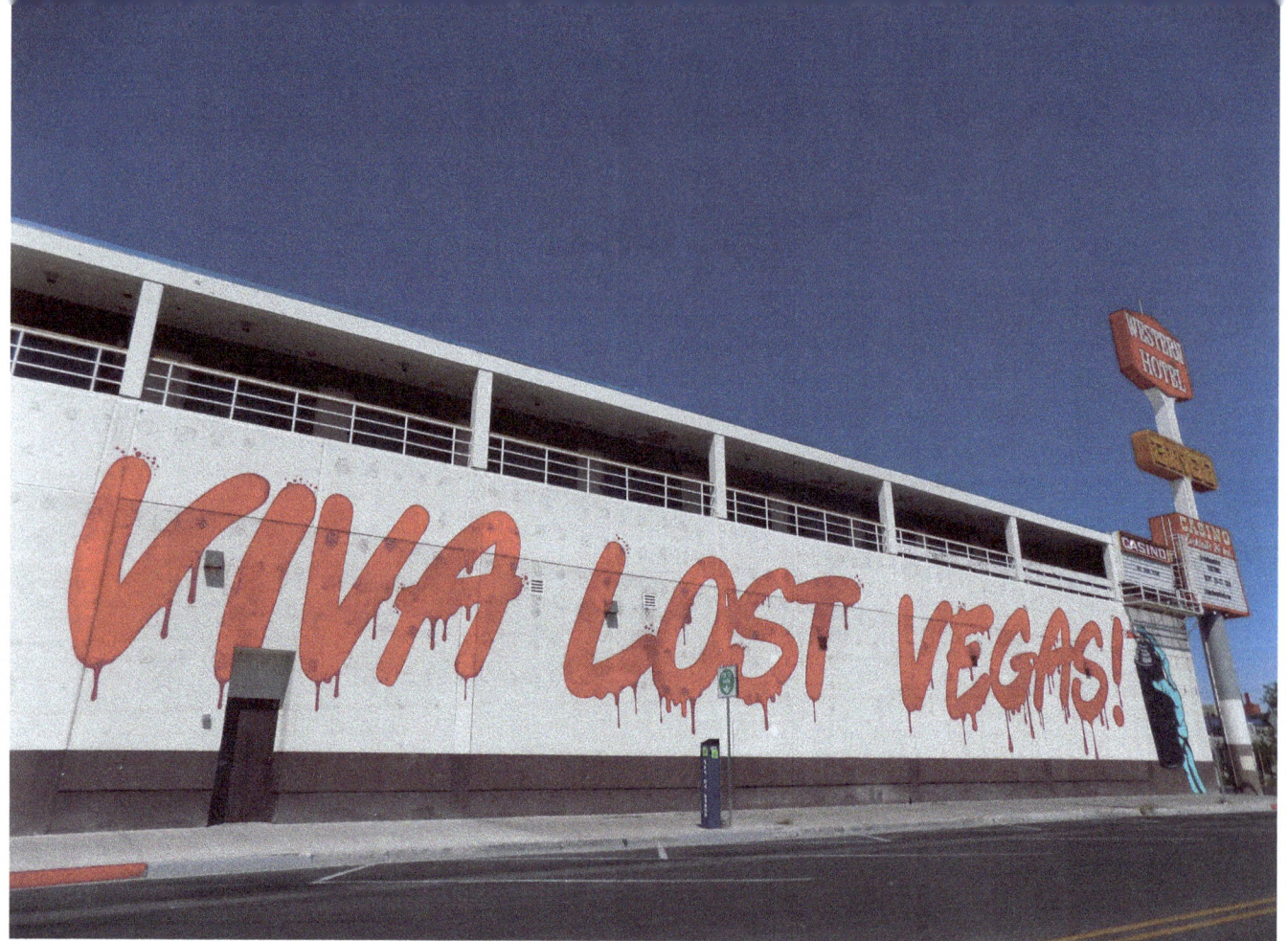

While the Great Recession has definitely done a number on Las Vegas, one thing remains certain: Vegas will bounce back. Once the fastest-growing major city in America, it will again see a resurgence. While not as quickly as other cities burdened by the Recession, Las Vegas is already rebounding.

As the saying goes, when one door closes, another opens. The real estate market is improving. While prices on residential and commercial properties may not be as low as they were when the market bottomed out, they are currently nowhere near the costly high of the boom days. This presents savvy investors and prospective homeowners with a unique opportunity to take advantage of deals that likely won't last forever. And established companies and small businesses looking to get their start now have many affordable options available to them. It's already happening. Like the days of the Old West, prospectors are coming to stake their turf, and the city is experiencing a rebirth. Just like the mythological phoenix, Las Vegas is rising from the ashes.

Millions from around the world visit Las Vegas every year and take part in the excitement offered by the Strip. That unique and vibrant experience, coupled with the unparalleled beauty of the desert and its pristine lakes and stunning, majestic mountains just minutes away, make Las Vegas a one-of-a-kind, truly special place. I, for one, am proud to now call it home.

Viva Las Vegas!

# *also available from the author*

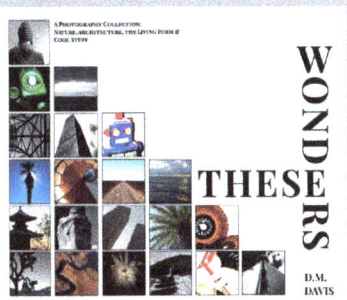
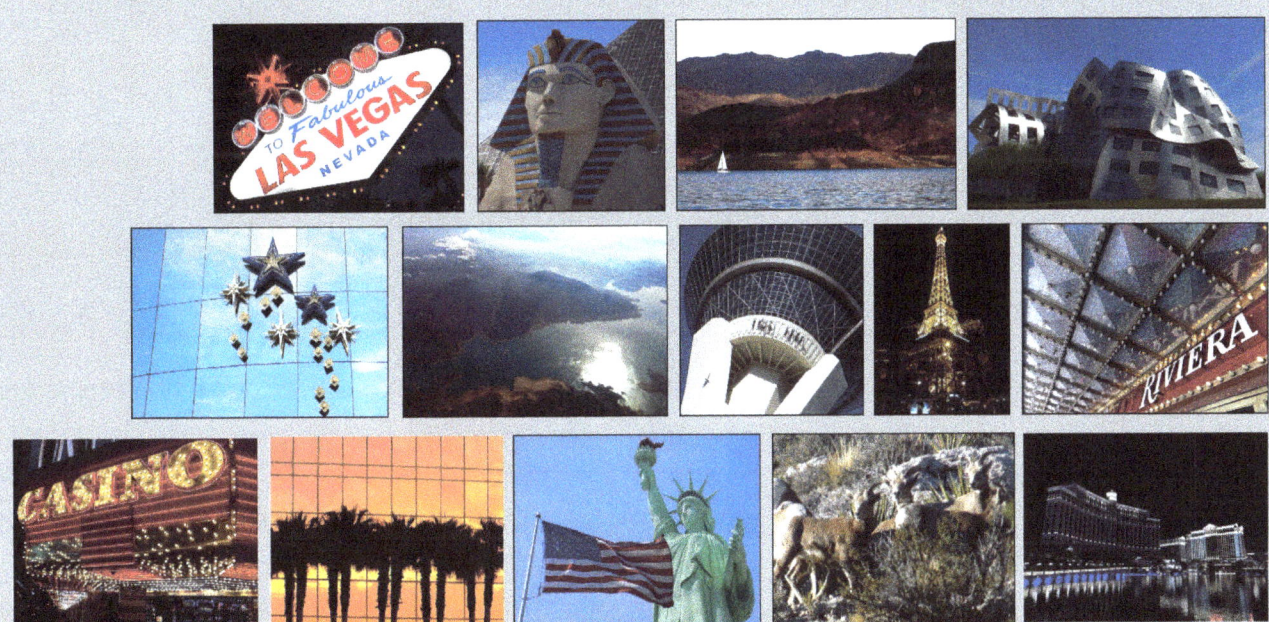
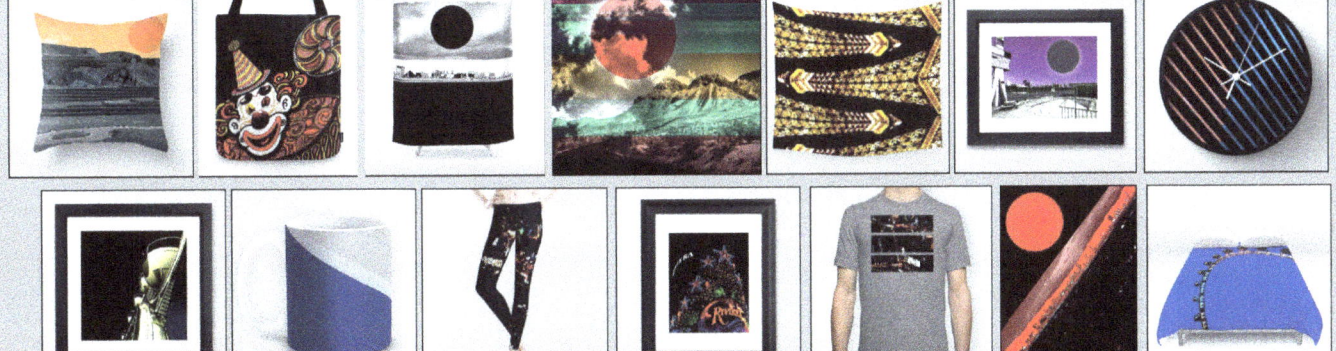

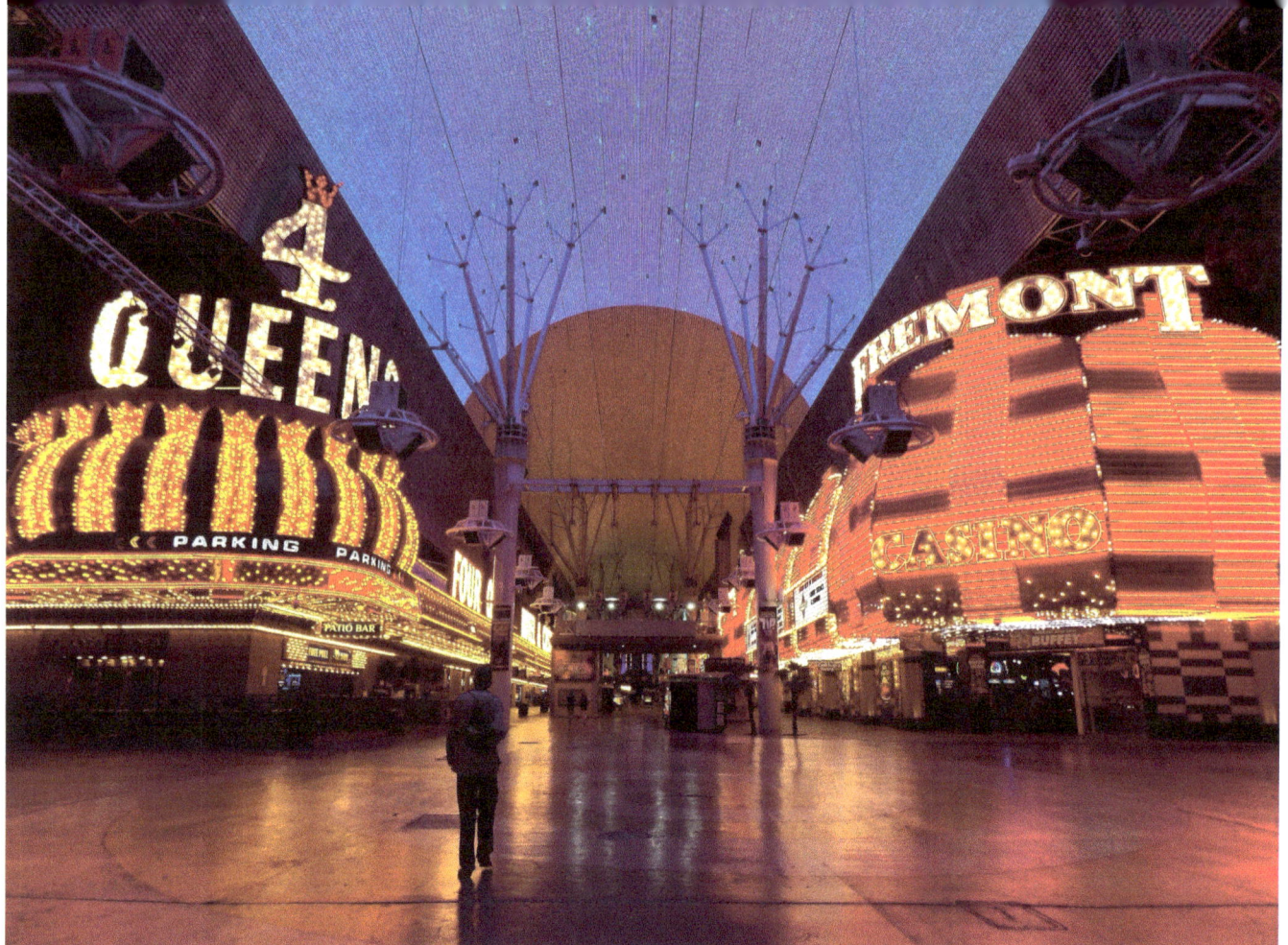

**Above:** A homeless man walks the sparsely populated late-night at the downtown Las Vegas Fremont Street Experience.

**Cover Image:** Shot from the vacant lot formerly home to the razed New Frontier Hotel & Casino,from left to right, the stalled Echelon sits forgotten, the Fontainebleau looms abandoned, and the Riviera's neon lights are now forever turned off.

All photography featured in *Abandoned: Lost Vegas* © D.M. Davis.

www.ingramcontent.com/pod-product-compliance
Lightning Source LLC
Chambersburg PA
CBHW041921180526